WITH NO REGRETS

With No Regrets

AN AUTOBIOGRAPHY

Krishna Nehru

Hutheesing
=

◆

'And time remember'd is grief forgotten'

An Asia Press Book

The John Day Company · New York

To

RAJA—MY HUSBAND

Illustrations follow
Page Sixteen

FOREWORD

I seldom consent to write a foreword, but as I have known Krishna Hutheesing since she was a child, I readily conceded her claim for my blessing on her sheaf of memories.

She undertook this book, she tells us, to solace the loneliness of those long anxious months following on the black Sunday of August 1942 that saw so many national workers, including almost her entire family, in prison.

With characteristic directness and complete candor, she recounts the tale of her own young life—for she is still quite young. She speaks of her happy if wayward childhood in a home of wealth and beauty, of her somewhat difficult and sometimes rebellious girlhood in surroundings strangely and unbelievably altered by the influence of the meek but oh! how mighty Mahatma, from a background of rich festivities to a battle camp of austere conflict and tremendous sacrifice. She gives us glimpses of her stay in Switzerland with an ailing sister-in-law, her travels with her father and brother in France and England, Germany and Russia, and mentions some famous people whom she met. She relates her experiences as a Satyagrahi prisoner in a women's jail, and confides in us the romance of her unconventional courtship and marriage, her reactions to new modes of living in new cities and unfamiliar environments; she presents to us her two small sons, Harsha and Ajit, for whose sakes she has been persuaded to refrain from an active share in the current political movement. Here and there the leaves are stained with tears of bereavement for father, mother and others dearly loved.

But this very personal narrative is closely woven into the

7

fabric of the family history of the Nehrus. Therein, for the wider public, will lie its special value and appeal. Has the history of the Nehrus not been for a quarter of a century both a living symbol and an integral part of the story of the Indian struggle for freedom?

In this simple and intimate chronicle, we discover the magnificent Motilal Nehru—where shall we ever find his equal?—in his most endearing and delightful role as the benevolent and genial patriarch and dictator of an adoring family, whom he loved with a surpassing devotion which impressed Mahatma Gandhi as the most remarkable of his many great qualities.

Here, Jawaharlal, that passionate and intrepid crusader for world causes, doffs his armor and sheathes his fiery sword, and proves himself an incomparable exponent of many-sided relationships as son and brother, husband, father, friend and perfect playmate of little children.

Here, too, drawn in tender colors, is the portrait of Jawahar's lovely and heroic wife, Kamala, the pathos of whose brief life and the poignant tragedy of whose death have already passed into lyric and legend in the country.

Swarup, now called Vijayalakshmi, winds her way through the pattern of this tale like a gleaming thread of silver; and Indira floats before our eyes for a moment, a delicate vision in her saffron bridal robes.

But to me most precious, perhaps, of all is the remembrance of that tiny and exquisite, aged and suffering woman, Motilal's wife, Jawahar's mother, in whom love and faith wrought so sweet a miracle of courage and endurance. She, who was carefully cherished and jealously guarded like a jewel in an ivory casket throughout her fragile youth and middle years, transformed herself in her frail old age into a gem-like flame of inspiration to guide those whose feet were set irrevocably on the steep and perilous paths of freedom.

Precious, too, is the pendant picture of that older sister, widowed in childhood, who dedicated her life to the tireless service of the Nehru household, and who, having fulfilled her last duties to her sister, laid down her life within twenty-four hours after she died—undivided in death as in life.

Across the landscape of this moving family history fall the bright lights and the half lights, the dimmer and the deeper shadows inseparable from human destiny.

The printed word ends here, but the living story of the Nehrus continues. The high traditions of patriotism created by an illustrious father and an illustrious son will be duly honoured by the younger generations that succeed them.

SAROJINI NAIDU

INTRODUCTION

Great paintings need spare framing; the relevant beauty of the wood draws the eye nearer to the canvas and not to itself. Krishna Hutheesing adds occasional commentary, as a marginal setting, to reveal the depths of her narrative. The story is almost made to tell itself; it is the drama of a Great House, with characters who belong to history, as its inmates. But it is the history in which India lives, and which she is shaping today. The symbol of a million hearts, this House of Joy—Anand Bhawan—stands as a radiating centre of movements which have swept the land, and the creative abundance it has released easily transcends the sufferings of an awakened people. We have pictures with garden and laughter, of the morning hours; the full blaze of a united popular will falls on its crowded precincts; tragic and momentous events proceed in a people's destiny, and the house is strangely astir. There are pictures also of stillness and hushed hours, with blinds drawn upon intimate bereavements some of which yet were shared by a nation. In offering her devotion, a daughter of the house takes us to the courtyard and the corridors; we have glimpses of rooms in which deeds are being shaped with courage and self-searching; homely details no less than the intellectual atmosphere are given to us with precise art; and even when we leave the gates, we are never far from the spot to which this book has endeared us.

Fully portrayed here are figures of the father and the son. They are world-known, but it was left for the author to make them so real and so human to us, with a familiar light denied to outsiders. No finer, truer art could have come to the aid of a writer than the touch of profound kinship and knowledge with which she has handled the theme. Through wonderful letters, memoried conversation, and quick transcript of events she tells us about her father and her brother, and brings her narrative down to the present day, when less is allowed to be told about them than ever before. Perhaps it is our sense of this intolerable obscuration which gives to each word about Jawaharlal Nehru an inexpressible glow; we read extracts from his recent letters, incomparable in their majesty and forgiveness, and in their sheer artistic power, with poignant delight.

But there are many unforgettable portraits in this book; the most tender and distinguished being those of the mother and of the aunt whom the author has adored. They live in the great house forever, enshrined in our imagination. A number of brilliant sketches, apart from those of family members, live in the context of the author's most significant experiences.

Strangely enough, this is not a political book even though, in a sense, it is nothing but that. This is so, perhaps, because politics, when it becomes one with our creative being, ceases to be merely political. It cannot then be viewed apart, or given a doctrinal or eventful significance. Of events and incidents there are plenty in this book; act by act they unfold even as India's destiny is enacted on the stage of our national civilization. But they are never related extraneously; occasions which have shaken the whole country seem to appear inevitably in the setting of this chronicle. When millions are sharing an epical existence, and heroism is a daily event, political sensationalism and dire threats are shamed into inconsequence. This is particularly true of a family in which dedicated lives have accepted uttermost trials and responsibilities, both individual and national, as part of a daily prerogative. Even when Krishna Hutheesing speaks on crucial issues, she preserves an "innocent eye," a detachment that can only come with the completest identification with the larger national purpose; so much so, that she can speak naturally about it. Her anger glows, and profound conviction welds her phrases as she opposes wrongs done to individuals and to a whole people; but so complete is her absorption in the inward humanity of events that readers, whose minds are immediately won, would hardly consider isolated facts excepting in strict relevance to an autobiographical narration.

An example of the author's power in fusing external episodes and an intimate personal sense of them is the description of the Lucknow Central Prison. There she spent many months in company with unfortunate sisters who were detained not for the crime of loving one's motherland and for serving one's fellow beings with the purest love and disinterestedness, but for actual crimes of violence. The story takes on a sublimity of pure expression; what the author sees, what she feels, her intellectual analysis of the complex issues involved in the present stage of our civilized sub-humanity, are all given but in a form which cannot be repeated and, therefore, must be read in the book. Politics, or sociology, call it what you will, is there, as it must be, but the story of Bachuli easily transcends the false divisions by which we classify principles and objectives in order to escape from a total human response. A darkened soul, crushed and then banished by a callous, irresponsible social order, calls to us. Correlated, remedial measures and not retaliation, we feel, would be the answer that even a partially humanized society could give. The high, jutting walls close upon the scene; the author takes a last look at the iron gates behind which dim figures would live out their years; the road outside, which her reluctant steps must pursue, becomes for the moment unreal. The whole picture attains the validity of a concrete, universal experience. What the author does for aftercare and penal reform, though full success cannot attend her efforts, lights up an area of our responsibility.

The reader will be grateful that this is a book of living lines, with the warm-tinted impressions of an artist who cares less to be competent than expressive. The writing, therefore, carries an air of improvisation, and an asymmetry which is never quite removed from living things. Arguments have not been drilled to precision angles; they are, indeed, there by implication. Neither has all available material been collected or scheduled. The story carries the rhythm of an inner adventure, the scenes shift from one page to another, and the method of reminiscent reflection seems entirely adequate for enjoyment. How delightful that she can tell us of her wanderings in Europe; her work and escapades and artistic hobbies; that she can write about her own children and home and reveal a little of her husband's self-effacing life of service, giving us the sense of a secret shared together. For all this and more, the reader of this autobiography will feel grateful.

A beautiful picture in a simple frame: that is how we shall view this book. There is no reason why new and other types of pictures by the same hand will not be added—indeed, this story raises such an expectation. Artistically, this book is complete; but many of the lives which form its subject will continue to annex noble chapters to themselves, and these chapters will also belong to an entire India and new humanity. When the sequel is written, as we hope it shall be, the blind mist which has been deliberately created to blacken the most sacred reputations will be dispelled. Clearer skies will allow details to be revealed regarding truths which no machine-ridden furies have been able to suppress. We shall welcome back, not to our hearts where they are already installed, but to our homes, numerous individuals who by their striving for great human ideals, and by an unremitting personal sacrifice for the reconciliation of adverse forces, have illumined the path of future civilization. But in our pain, and in our spiritual awakening, we shall today read this book and gather sustenance—the sustenance that the example of the supreme builder of the age, now suffering for us all, and the story of noble lives inspired by his unflinching moral purpose, have offered to a distracted mankind. This autobiographical record is a testimony to the faith which is inseparable from action, and which is in the words of Rabindranath, "the supreme courage of love."

AMIYA CHAKRAVARTY

13

ABOUT THIS BOOK

Some years ago my husband asked me to write the book I had often thought of writing, but I did not attempt it then. In March 1941 when Raja was imprisoned and I was left on my own, I decided to make an effort. I had written a couple of chapters when my elder son got typhoid and I could not carry on with my writing. Raja was released and we spent many anxious months while our child was ill. After he recovered I could not settle down to work at my book again.

Over a year passed. Raja was back in prison for an unknown period and I was left alone once again. The first few months were difficult and unsettled and it was not easy to adjust one's mind to any sort of work, but gradually one got used to new conditions. As the hours dragged heavily on my hands I decided to start on my book afresh. Being able to write down all the thoughts and memories that came flooding over me has in some measure helped to make these long lonely months a little less lonesome and more bearable. I have sorely missed my husband's guidance and my brother's rather stern criticism which I would gladly have welcomed. But it could not be. Had it not been for a friend of ours who always found time to help me in revising and giving valuable suggestions, I should not have been able to complete the work so quickly. His help, advice and never flagging interest have been of immense help to me, especially during those days when, dejected and depressed beyond words, I did not feel like working at all.

I am deeply grateful to Dr. Amiya Chakravarty, or "Amiya da" as I call him, whom I consider my "guru." For years he, too, has been asking me to write a book of reminiscences, but

I felt I could not do so. His unwavering faith in my ability to write made me somewhat nervous. Though I did not take his advice, Amiya da persisted with the idea every time he wrote to me; and from within the gloomy walls of Yeravda Prison, Raja also encouraged me. So I undertook the task though not without a certain amount of hesitation.

Amiya da has done me the honor of writing the introduction to my book. For this as well as for all the encouragement and guidance he gave me I owe him a deep debt of gratitude.

To Mrs. Sarojini Naidu also are due my grateful thanks for having written the foreword in spite of being far from well. I have known her for a very long time and her friendship and deep affection for my family is well known.

My thanks are also due to the *Statesman* for permitting me to reproduce the story of "Bachuli," to the *Hindu* for Chapter 17 and to *Visvabharati* for Chapter 18; all of which have appeared in their columns some time ago.

I felt I could not do so. His unwavering faith in my ability to write made me somewhat nervous. Though I did not take his advice, Amiya da persisted with the idea every time he wrote to me; and from within the gloomy walls of Yaravda Prison, Raja also encouraged me. So I undertook the task though not without a certain amount of hesitation.

Amiya da has done me the honor of writing the introduction to my book. For this as well as for all the encouragement and guidance he gave me I owe him a deep debt of gratitude. To Mrs. Sarojini Naidu also are due my grateful thanks for having written the foreword in spite of being far from well, I have known her for a very long time and her friendship and deep affection for my family is well known.

My thanks are also due to the Statesman for permitting me to reproduce the story of "Bachuli," to the Hindu for Chapter 17 and to Vishbharati for Chapter 18; all of which have appeared in their columns some time ago.

Krishna Nehru Hutheesing

Raja Hutheesing, Krishna's husband

Anand Bhawan, the Nehrus' famous house, which has been given to the nation and is now called Swaraj Bhawan

Motilal Nehru, Krishna's father

Rani Nehru, Krishna's mother

Jawaharlal Nehru

Swarup (Vijayalakshmi Pandit), Krishna's sister

Indira Nehru, Jawaharlal's daughter

I.

No, it is not yet night,
Two or three are still standing guard;
But it is growing damned dark and perhaps
They, the watchmen, too, will be slaughtered
Before they see the morning.

—PIERRE VAN PAASSEN

On August 9th 1942 at precisely 5 a.m. the Bombay
police paid us a surprise visit armed with warrants of arrest for
Jawahar and Raja. After many days of strenuous activity, due
to the meetings of the All India Congress Committee, we were
all rather weary and fagged out. Till late at night all of us had
been talking and discussing recent happenings. At midnight
our guests departed and Jawahar, Raja and I sat on talking for
another hour. Then we went to bed.

To be waked up so early after a late night was bad enough,
but to find the police on one's door-step was anything but
pleasant. Fast asleep though I was when the door-bell rang, I
woke up at once and I did not have to be told that the police
had arrived. No one else would come at that ungodly hour
except the police. I hurried to Jawahar's room, as I thought the
warrant was only for him. Terribly tired, he could hardly keep
his eyes open, nor could he collect his drowsy senses together.
Within a few minutes the whole house was awake and when
we had fully realized that the inevitable had happened we set
about to help Jawahar get packed. Raja was also helping to get
some books together when my niece Indira said, "Raja bhai,
why aren't you getting ready?" I turned round sharply and
asked, "What for?" "There is a warrant for him, too," Indira
told us. Somehow we did not imagine that anyone except the

members of the Working Committee would be arrested in the first round-up, but we were mistaken!

So Raja also got his things together and all too soon they were ready to go. We bade farewell to them and they were escorted to their respective cars by the police officials; Jawahar to an unknown destination and Raja to Yeravda Central Prison, Poona. We waved goodby and returned to the flat wondering what the future had in store for all of us this time.

We had many guests staying with us then and the flat was full to overflowing. Only two persons had gone away and yet everything seemed changed. Something was lacking, something vital had gone which seemed to have made the place alive before and barren and deserted now. For days the house had been full of people coming and going, and the stream of visitors continued now in an even increasing number. Friends, relatives and war correspondents of all kinds and descriptions hovered around for details of the arrests. Still we missed those that had gone away and our thoughts were with them constantly.

Many a time the same thing had happened, but one could not get accustomed to it. Each time it left one a little bewildered and a little lonely.

For a year now, those near and dear to me have been away, imprisoned behind grim walls and iron bars. Even sight of them has been denied. But their absence, though creating a great void in my life, does not make me despair or falter. I am convinced that the cause for which they have been incarcerated is a just and right one and that that they must suffer for it is inevitable.

A year is not a very long time in the life of an individual, much less in the life of a nation. But sometimes the year lengthens itself out and each month seems to be an enormous period of time. I have gone through several great movements and who knows how many more one might still have to face. Throughout all these years not only I but countless numbers of our comrades have gone through periods of varying emotions. We have experienced moments of great exultation and moments of great depression. Sometimes we have been surrounded by shadows and darkness, unable to find a way out. At other times, streaks of light have pierced the darkness that enveloped us and given us new hope and courage to carry on with our struggle.

During all these months of chaos and loneliness many memories have come crowding into my mind. Just to keep my mind occupied, I started scribbling them down and gradually these memories and reminiscences have taken the shape of a book. Writing it, I have relived many of the days of my childhood and onwards. They have been pleasant memories and sad ones, and I have laughed as well as wept over many an incident of days gone by. They have given me some pleasure, a great deal of peace and often a little heartache.

During my childhood I had lived a serene peaceful life. We were a small, compact family and our little world was a happy one, untouched by sorrow or hardships. Gradually our lives had to undergo many changes; but we remained together, so nothing mattered. As time passed, force of circumstances made us scatter. But life went on and we continued to live, adapting ourselves to new ways and new methods and making ourselves mentally and physically stronger to face whatever might come our way.

A few months ago—ten months, to be exact—I wrote to Jawahar "somewhere in India" and commented on all the changes that had taken place in our family during the last fifteen years. His reply gives a vivid picture of all that was, is and may be, and shows how life affected us. Yet in spite of the odds we have had to fight against, we do not regret anything. He writes:—

"You write of 1928 and of our compact family then: now many of our loved ones are dead and the others scattered and isolated, unable even to see each other. That lesson repeated in each generation has to be learnt by each generation through personal experience. Integration follows disintegration, but

19

each integration is perhaps on a higher level than the previous one, for it carries subconsciously somewhere the memory of past successes and failures. The burden of the past pursues us, and yet it is both a burden and an inspiration, for it drags us down and at the same time pushes us on. Sometimes we feel vital and youthful and full of energy; at other times thousands of years weigh us down and we feel old and a little weary at this long and interminable pilgrimage. Both are part of us and make us what we are and out of that ceaseless intermingling and conflict something new is always arising. We, who are children of ancient civilizations with hundreds of passionate generations behind us with all their struggles and contentment, their dynamics and statics, feel this more than people of a later day who have not these complex pasts pursuing them. We have much that gives an equilibrium to the mind and spirit, a calm and unhurried outlook on life which refuses to get flurried and flustered at changing events. That essentially is the hallmark of ancient culture; it is that, that China has in abundant measure; it is this, I believe, that India also possesses. And because of this, it will be well with India.

"When I was a child, I remember our family consisting of twenty persons or more, all living together as joint families do. I saw that large family disintegrate and then each part form itself into a nucleus of integration; and yet silken bonds of affection and common interests joined those separate parts and there was always an integration of the large whole. That process continues and normally you would hardly notice it, but when events hasten it, there is a shock. Think of what happened in China during the past five years and of the cataclysm that has overwhelmed hundreds of thousands of families. Yet the nation lives, more vital than ever, and individuals are born and grow and carry on the tradition of the race and humanity in spite of war and catastrophe. I sometimes feel that we in India would be the better for some such mass experience. Anyway, we are having our own experience and thus building up slowly but surely a new nation."

2.

Verse, a breeze 'mid blossoms straying
Where hope clung feeding like a bee
Both were mine! Life went a-maying
With Nature, Hope and Poesy
When I was young.

—COLERIDGE

It was a bitterly cold morning in November 1907 when I was born in the sacred City of Prayaga or Allahabad as it is now known. The whole house was lit up brightly and humming with activity even at a fairly late hour of the night, for my mother was having rather a bad time and everybody was anxiously awaiting the birth of the baby. After a great deal of trouble I was born, a big, fat, healthy infant, little realizing that I had almost cost my frail little mother her life in the very process of coming into this world. For weeks afterwards my mother hovered between life and death, while, left to the tender mercies of nurses and others, I thrived as a normal baby should.

Mother recovered slowly, but remained a semi-invalid for a long time. It was hardly possible for her to look after me. So I continued to be cared for by nurses and an aunt of mine. When I was about three years old, the English governess who looked after my sister Swarup took charge of me also. My brother Jawahar is eighteen years older than I and my sister seven years older. So I grew up almost like an only child with no companionship, nor anything in common with my brother or sister. The former I did not even know as he was away in England when I was born, and I first made my acquaintance with him when I was five years old.

When I was born my father had already made a name for himself as a great lawyer and was a wealthy man. Father bought Anand Bhawan, our home, when Jawahar was ten years old. The site on which it stands is supposed to be very sacred, as it presumed to have been the place where Rama and Bharat met when the former returned from his fourteen years' exile. Nearby is the Bharadwaj Ashram, where in ancient days there used to be a university, and which is still a place of pilgrimage.

Our house always attracted crowds, especially during the great Kumbh Mela, held every twelve years in Prayaga. Lakhs of people flocked to the sacred city to bathe in the "sangam." During this time the crowds that visited our house were so large that it was impossible to control them and they used to scatter all over the compound where they rested for a while. Every year smaller crowds came on their pilgrimage to attend the Magh Mela. Few returned to their villages or towns without visiting our home. They came partly because it was a sacred place and partly through curiosity, to have a look at the people they had heard so much about, like Father and Jawahar.

Anand Bhawan is a large rambling house with big verandahs all round and a huge garden. On one side of the house was a lawn, at the back a fruit garden, in front was a long stretch of another garden with a summer house and a tennis court. Inside the summer house was an image of Shiva placed high on the large stones, which were placed one on top of the other to make it look like a miniature mountain. From Shiva's head a tiny stream trickled down into a pool at the foot of it, and lovely flowers grew all around. In summer this place was delightfully cool and I loved it. Later on, when our new house was built, the summer house was demolished as it obstructed the new building.

Father had many horses, dogs, cars and carriages and was very fond of hunting and riding. I used to love strolling around the stables and looking at the horses. I had my own pony—a beautiful snow-white creature for whom many people had offered Father large sums of money but with whom Father refused to part. I did not keep him long, for one day he died in his stable—bitten by a snake. It was a terrible tragedy for me, as I loved him dearly, and for many weeks I grieved over his loss.

During my childhood we almost always had relatives staying with us. Sometimes there were children, too, and I enjoyed having them to play with. I marvelled how Mother, even from her sick bed, could look after all the people in the house and how Father, in spite of all his work, could find time to spend a few minutes with each and every one and see that they were comfortable and happy. He was like a shepherd who, though apparently unconcerned, kept a vigilant eye on all his flock, and he did it to perfection.

Some years before I was born, there had been a little son who had not lived, and Mother had never reconciled herself to his loss. When I was born a girl, my mother was sorely disappointed, but to Father it made little difference. I had a strange lonely childhood with few playmates. Adhering to strict rules and regulations, every minute of my life was planned out from the minute I woke up to the time I went to bed. I resented it very much, more so because other children I knew were allowed more freedom by their parents and had no governess to lay down hard and fast rules. I resented the authority which my governess exercised over me, and very often I disobeyed her, for I not only was stubborn, but had rather a wild temper which more often than not got the better of me. It is quick to get roused, but fleeting and childish. It seldom lasts for a long time and holds no malice, but it frequently leads me into a great deal of unnecessary trouble!

To be punished, locked up alone or deprived of my supper was a frequent occurrence with me; but it rarely happened to my sister. She was always obedient and docile, most probably because it was less troublesome to obey than to disobey. Yet in spite of my resentment and my tantrums, I loved my governess deeply and I knew she was very fond of me too.

23

As a child I saw very little of my parents. Father was always very busy and I saw him only for a short while in the mornings and again in the evenings. I saw Mother more often, but did not have much to do with her. When she was well, Mother could never sit quietly, and always had to be doing some house-work in spite of a fleet of servants waiting to carry out her smallest commands. I loved her very much and worshipped her loveliness, but many a time my childish heart grieved because I felt she did not care for me as much as I should have liked her to.

Jawahar, my brother, was the apple of her eye and she made no secret of her love for him. Father was no less proud and fond of Jawahar and maybe he was even more so than Mother, but he was less demonstrative about it, as he had a tremendous sense of justice and fairness and he did not want any one of us to feel that another was a favorite. In this he succeeded. Yet, constantly hearing a great deal in praise of Jawahar, I became rather jealous of him, and was not sorry that he was away from home.

My sister Swarup was very lovely and was spoiled by everybody, but somehow of her I was never jealous. I took it for granted that anyone so beautiful as she was should naturally be made much of, and I was exceedingly fond of her.

My childhood was one of clock-like regularity. I started the day by going for a ride every morning, which I loved and still do to this day. Father was a fine horseman and had a good stable. All three of us, Jawahar, Swarup and I, learned to ride almost as soon as we learned to walk and we were all very fond of it, though we rarely get a chance to ride now. After my ride, I had lessons with my governess in a corner of our enormous garden. The whole morning thus passed until lunch time. After lunch I had to rest—a most annoying process—then a piano lesson and some more lessons to end up with. In the evening we went out for a drive every day, in a carriage drawn by two Burmese ponies which were the pride of my father's heart.

For the rest, the evenings were usually dull. Cinemas were

not in fashion as they are today and I was very rarely permitted to see one. An occasional visit to a circus or a fair was considered more than enough. Today my own little sons, seven and eight years old, know more about both Indian and American films than I knew at the age of twelve. Sometimes I had a few friends to play with but not often. So I amused myself roaming about the spacious grounds of our home, wondering a great deal about life in general and always keeping my thoughts to myself. For I had learned at an early age that "children should be seen and not heard," and being inquisitive or asking too many questions was a sign of bad manners! So I never got an outlet to express myself, and although my head was full of hundreds of questions that I was aching to ask, I did not have the chance to do so.

Swarup was five years old when she went to England with our parents and it was there that Father had engaged our governess, Miss Hooper. She was a very fine person with extremely good qualifications and came from a very good family. She belonged to the old school which believed in stern discipline and unswerving obedience. Swarup was easy to handle, but I, having inherited all the stubbornness not only of my father but also of a long line of ancestors, was quite a problem. No punishment was severe enough to make me give in, and yet one gentle reproof was sufficient to make me ashamed of myself and to be only too eager to do as I was asked. Unfortunately reproofs were rare and punishments frequent. Thus I grew up from a lonely child to an awkward shy girl, longing to be made much of, hungering for knowledge, but never attaining it except by the beaten track. My parents remained more or less strangers to me and my brother I did not know at all. My sister was the only person with whom I came in contact daily, apart from my governess, whom I adored and hated by turns.

The first great event in my life was the return of my brother from England in 1912. He was a complete stranger to me, and though I felt no joy at the prospect of his home-coming, I was curious to see what he was like. Weeks before his arrival my parents were busy making preparations to welcome home their son and heir. Mother was unable to conceal her joy and lived in a fever of excitement—she rushed backwards and forwards all day long, seeing that all was in perfect order for the beloved son. I remember how happy she looked during these days—how her face glowed with a radiance I had never seen before. It irritated me sometimes beyond measure that my mother should dote thus on a mere son! Today I understand so well how she felt at that time. Even my sister flitted about the house with an air of eager expectancy which was most exasperating to me. I made up my mind to dislike Jawahar thoroughly.

At last the great day arrived and the atmosphere of suppressed excitement throughout the house affected even me, but only with more curiosity. It was summer and we were in the hill station, Mussoorie. At the expected hour we heard horses' hoofs clattering up the drive, and everybody ran outside to meet Jawahar. My heart sank a little when I saw a handsome young man, so very like Mother to look at, ride up towards us. He jumped down from his horse. First he embraced Mother, then greeted all the others in turn. I stood at a distance trying to make up my mind whether or not to like the new brother who had suddenly descended on us. While many thoughts crowded in my mind I was lifted in Jawahar's arms and heard him say, "So this is the baby sister? She is quite a little lady now." He kissed me and put me down as abruptly as he had picked me up—then forgot all about me the very next minute.

The first few months of our acquaintanceship were anything but pleasant. Jawahar was an awful tease, for when he had nothing to do, he spent his time playing pranks on me. He made me do all sorts of things I most disliked or feared. When I least expected it he would shower me with gifts and be exceedingly sweet, so that it was not possible to remain annoyed with him for long. Even so I remained aloof and did not grow very fond of him.

The first World War did not affect my quiet and sometimes monotonous life. The only change I found in our household was that Mother went more often to clubs and sat with a lot of Indian and foreign women knitting things for soldiers. I also noticed Father and Jawahar getting very agitated over some war news every now and then.

In 1916 Jawahar married. For months preparations had been going on, for the wedding was to be held with great pomp and splendor. The house was full of jewellers, merchants and tailors coming in and out throughout the day, and numerous clerks were busy planning out details and making arrangements.

The marriage was to take place in Delhi, the bride's home, and the bridegroom's party left Allahabad a week before the wedding day, on a day that was considered auspicious. Father took more than a hundred guests with him and we went by a special train which was beautifully decorated. Hundreds of other guests joined us in Delhi. As even several houses could not hold our guests, father had numerous tents put up for everyone and in a week's time a little colony of tents cropped up. It was called the "Nehru Wedding Camp."

Delhi was bitterly cold in those days, but I loved it and had a grand time. Many cousins whom I had not seen before came from all parts of India and I enjoyed playing with them. Each day there was a party somewhere or other, and after ten days the wedding party returned to Allahabad where there were some more festivities.

Jawahar made a handsome bridegroom and Kamala was one of the loveliest brides I have ever seen. In November 1917 their only daughter, Indira, was born.

Life was uneventful till 1917. That year my governess got engaged to an English friend of hers and wanted to get married fairly soon. All her people were in England; so Father naturally offered to give her away in church. I was greatly excited at the prospect of a wedding and of acting bridesmaid, but I was also unhappy at the idea of parting from my governess. All the things I disliked about her were forgotten. I remembered only the love and care she had lavished on me for all those years. She had been with us for twelve long years and was looked upon as one of our family. We were all very fond of her and she in her turn was devoted to us.

The wedding day dawned and I was miserable. Everything went off beautifully and she was very pleaseed with all that Father had done for her. After the wedding she left on her honeymoon and I was inconsolable for days. It was the first heartbreak of my young life. But childish griefs pass quickly and I got used to her absence. Soon I began to enjoy my newly acquired freedom, for I could do more or less as I liked, and was left to my own resources a great deal.

I had always wanted to go to school and study with other children, but my father had never approved of the idea. He thought it was the correct thing to have lessons in solitary grandeur with a governess. The necessary qualifications for a young lady in those days were to be able to play the piano or some other musical instrument, and to carry on a conversation and mix well in society. My sister had never been to school and had been educated at home. But I do not think she ever wished to go, whereas I did.

When our governess got married I tried hard to persuade Father to allow me to join school. At first he was adamant and wanted me to have another governess. Several of them came, but fortunately they did not stay. At last Father gave in very grudgingly and I went to school. The school that was chosen for me was supposed to be just the right thing—a very select little place for young ladies and little men. There were mostly English children before I joined, but later many Indian children joined it, too.

It was the beginning of a new life for me and I enjoyed every minute of it. Games and studies took up all my time and I never had time to feel lonely any more. Life seemed too good to be true and some of the happiest days of my childhood were my school days. After a few short years, they came to a rather abrupt end.

And so I grew up in an atmosphere of security and peace in a home I adored.

3.

Ah! for a change 'twixt Now and Then!

—COLERIDGE

Since the departure of our governess, Swarup had looked after me, as Mother was too delicate to do so. She was seldom strict with me and more often than not I did just as I pleased. That was less trouble for her and it suited me. I was very fond of poetry and so was she. Many a delightful evening we spent sitting in the garden, she reading aloud and I listening to her with rapt attention. A bond existed between us that was rare and beautiful. Swarup was my guide, philosopher and friend during those days of my childhood.

In 1920 my sister was married. Her marriage was a very grand affair—done in the correct Kashmiri style. We had hundreds of guests, friends and relations staying with us as well as the entire Congress Working Committee which was holding one of its meetings in Allahabad. I had a gorgeous time during those days with hardly anyone to bother about me or tell me what to do or what not to do. I was unhappy at the idea of parting from my sister, but I was also delighted with the wedding festivities.

It was during these days that I decided to give up eating meat. I was very fond of it and one day Mahadeo Bhai Desai (Gandhiji's secretary) saw me having my lunch. He was quite upset at the sight of the different kinds of meat before me and there and then gave me a long sermon on becoming a vegetarian. I was not easily won over, but Mahadeo Bhai persisted day after day, whenever he caught sight of me. I gave it up in the midst of all the wedding festivities, much to the distress of everyone except my mother. She was overjoyed. She disliked meat and would never touch it of her own free will. During her illness she was forced to take soups or meat in some form or other. For three years I did not touch any meat, though I often longed for it. Then I went one Christmas to spend a week or so with some cousins. Seeing them all eat meat was too great a temptation and I succumbed!

After Swarup left home, I was rather miserable and lonely. There was, of course, my sister-in-law Kamala, who was of the same age as Swarup and in some ways she took Swarup's place.

It was at this time that I saw more of Father and got to know him better. He, too, guessing that I missed Swarup, gave me as much of his companionship as he could. I was just learning to know and love him more than I had ever done before when he was arrested for the first time and our brief period of companionship came to an abrupt end.

The first time I met Gandhiji was early in 1920. He had come to Allahabad at Father's request to have some discussions with him. I had heard much about 'Bapu,' as Gandhiji is called, but to me he seemed a mythical figure. I was very young and could not easily grasp all he stood for. His ideas seemed rather fantastic. When I saw him for the first time, I thought he was uninteresting. I had expected to see someone tall and strong with flashing eyes and a firm step. Instead I saw a thin, almost starved looking man, a little bent, wearing a loin-cloth and leaning on a stick, meek looking and very gentle. I was most disappointed. Was this the little man, I wondered, who was going to do great deeds for our country and free it from foreign domination?

I had heard and read much about the gruesome details of Jallianwala Bagh; and young though I was, I wanted to take

30

revenge. But to me revenge meant paying back in the same coin by violence and bloodshed. When I heard of Bapu's ideas of non-violence I thought that it was all moonshine and that no one, least of all a whole nation, could practice it. Besides, there is a streak of perversity in my nature and because nearly everyone I knew seemed to worship Bapu and existed to carry out his smallest behests, I put on an appearance of indifference which sorely grieved my mother. At heart I admired and loved Bapu, but I refused to treat him as others did, as a saint or a superman.

The more I saw of him, the more I was drawn towards him. At times he seemed to me to belong to a different sphere and yet he was very much of this earth and could appreciate things that are earthly. With his gentle eyes and winning smile, he won me over as he did millions of others, not for the moment only, but for our entire lives. For allegiance once given to Bapu, when given whole-heartedly, can never waver.

In 1920 Gandhiji launched the Satyagraha Movement and with its advent not only my life, but that of our entire family and of hundreds of others changed completely. One of the items of the movement was the boycott of British schools. I had been so absorbed with my studies and my own little world that I had hardly noticed the incoming storm or the changes that were taking place around me in my own home. So it came as rather a blow when Father sent for me one day and, having explained the situation, told me that I must leave school. I was attached to the school and had made many friends there. The idea of giving it up made me unhappy for a while, though I realized that that was the only right thing to do. It was not opportune to join another school just then, so Father arranged for tutors to come and teach me at home. For weeks I was unsettled and unhappy, having nothing much to do, but life moved fast in those days and soon I also got caught up in the whirlpool of events that were to change the very face of our country.

Something new happened every day to change my once dull

and monotonous life of strict routine into an ever-changing and exciting day to day existence, never knowing what was going to happen next. Jawahar wanted to join Gandhiji. My father wanted to think over all the pros and cons before he took the plunge. Jawahar's mind, however, was made up, and he pledged himself to the Satyagraha Movement. He did not do it without a great mental conflict. Jawahar felt that Satyagraha under Gandhiji's leadership was the only way to attain freedom. But it was no easy task to get Father to give his full consent to his joining Bapu. Father did not take to Gandhiji's ideas quickly and though he had given much consideration to the proposed movement, he did not like it very much. He did not then see any sense in going to prison and neither did he like the idea of Jawahar courting arrest. The pilgrimage to prison had not yet begun. Father loved Jawahar deeply and the very idea of his son having to suffer hardships and go to prison was far from pleasant.

For many days a conflict took place in both Jawahar's and Father's minds. There were long discussions and sometimes heated words. Both spent tortured days and nights trying each in his own way to convince the other. Father was distressed at Jawahar's determination to follow Bapu. We discovered later that he used to try sleeping on the floor to find out what it felt like, for he thought that that was what Jawahar would have to do! These were most unhappy days for all of us, especially for Mother and Kamala, who could not bear to see father and son torn by politics and endless arguments. The atmosphere was tense all the time and one hardly dared to utter a word for fear of rousing Father's anger or irritating Jawahar.

The happenings in the Punjab and the tragedy of Jallianwala Bagh however brought Father round to a great extent to Jawahar's way of thinking. It was then that his son's unswerving purpose and complete faith in the cause of Satyagraha as well as the great love he bore his only son, brought conviction to Father. He decided to throw in his lot with Jawahar and follow Gandhiji. But before doing so, he gave up his large practice at the bar. This changed our life, which until then had been of ease and luxury, to one of simplicity and a little hardship.

Father had earned millions and had also spent lavishly, never hoarding up money for a rainy day. When he gave up his practice, we immediately had to bring about certain changes in the household as it was not possible to live as we had been doing, with no income at all. The first thing Father did was to sell his horses and carriages. It was not easy for him to do this for he loved his horses dearly and was proud of them—but it had to be done. Then we had to dismiss quite a few of the army of servants we had and curtail expenses in every direction. There were no more banquets; only one cook instead of two or three, and no more smart butlers with numerous bearers as their satellites. All our lovely Dresden and Venetian china and glass and many other articles both expensive and beautiful were sold off and we had to get used to fewer servants and less of the luxuries of daily life. I was too young to really mind, but it must have been very hard on the others, especially my parents.

Just before all these changes occurred in our lives, a curious incident happened. We had many outhouses behind our house where coal, wood and other things used to be stored up. A huge cobra used to live in one of the outhouses where the wood was kept. Ever since I could remember it had been there. It molested no one and the servants went there unhesitatingly even late at night. Often the cobra could be seen gliding away along the garden or round about the outhouses. No one was scared or bothered about it. The popular superstition was that so long as it was there, guarding the interest of the family, no harm could come to our house, and only wealth and prosperity would be ours.

Sometime in 1920, just before Father gave up his practice, a new servant who did not know of the existence of the cobra saw it one evening. He got thoroughly scared and together with some others he killed it. All our old servants were horrified, and so was Mother; but the deed was done. Soon after-

33

wards, changes took place. Our luxurious home turned into a much simpler abode and Jawahar and Father went to prison. The servants attributed our bad luck, as they called it then, to the death of the cobra!

For my father, non-co-operation meant breaking away completely from his old life and trying to refashion it at the age of sixty. It meant a break not only from professional and political colleagues, but from life-long friends who could not see eye to eye with him or Bapu. It meant giving up many comforts. And he had always lived well. But once Father was convinced that this was the right path, he threw in his lot whole-heartedly and never gave the past a thought.

Each day Father and Jawahar got more and more immersed in politics. Our home where life had run so smoothly before was now always in a state of chaos. Numerous Congress workers came from all parts of the country to stay a few days and discuss matters. Meetings were held almost daily and there was a never-ending stream of people in and out of the house. I had always been used to a great many people visiting my parents, but they were of a different type. They came in smart cars or carriages drawn by lovely horses each vying with the other in showing off their pomp and splendor. After the movement started, quite a few of our wealthy friends kept away, and where one saw riches and wealth before, one now saw khadi-clad men and women, simple and humble. Each one bore within his or her heart an unconquerable determination, an undaunted courage to serve and free the country, and if need be, die for it.

In 1921 matters came to a head and the British Government started its campaign of wholesale arrests. Our people were prepared for it and rallied in their thousands. Prison until then was still something vague and unknown though very soon it was to become a second home to many of them.

At this time the Prince of Wales came to visit India and was due to visit Allahabad also. A few days before he came my father received a communication from the District Magistrate

34

of Allahabad calling upon him to allow the use of his grounds, and instructing him about the closing of the gates at a given time, admission of visitors etc. Father replied saying that the Magistrate had no authority over the use of his own property and he would make such use of it as he thought lawful and proper. Father assured him that as a non-co-operator he would see to it that no harm befell the Prince of Wales during his visit to Allahabad. For this assurance he was rewarded by being arrested. One evening we heard that there was going to be a general round-up and that all the leaders and prominent workers were going to be arrested. That same evening—it was the sixth of December 1921—the police paid their first visit to Anand Bhawan with warrants of arrest for Father and Jawahar. Since then they have come quite frequently, either to arrest some member of our family or to search the house for imaginary banned literature. More often they came to confiscate our cars and relieve us of a lot of surplus furniture in realization of fines.

The arrival of the police that evening caused quite a stir in our household. Some of the old servants were most indignant and wanted to beat up the police and throw them out of the compound. But Mother warned them not to behave stupidly. All of us were rather distressed at the suddenness of the arrests, all except Father and Jawahar. The idea of our loved ones being put behind prison bars worried us. We did not know what hardships were in store for them. It was hardest of all for my mother, to whom the past few months of constant change had been a sort of nightmare she had not quite fathomed. But she was a brave wife and a still more brave mother. On no account would she allow the others to see how wretched she felt at that moment.

Father and Jawahar got ready and bade us farewell. Then, entering the police car, they were driven away to the district jail. Mother and Kamala smiled bravely as they parted from their husbands, but though their smile was courageous, there were sadness and loneliness in their hearts. We turned back into the house when the car was out of sight, but the home that a moment ago had been so full of life suddenly seemed ever so quiet and bereft of all joy.

Father, Jawahar and others were tried on the seventh of December 1921, before the District Magistrate. The Government Advocate who opened the case for the prosecution was an Indian, a very old friend and comrade of Father's. He did not have the courage to refuse to prosecute Father or to resign his job, but I have never seen a man look more ashamed or nervous than he did during the trial. Throughout he kept his eyes averted and never once looked straight at Father. He conducted the proceedings in a low, almost inaudible voice. Before that, he used to meet Father almost every day—shared his hospitality and enjoyed all the privileges of a friend. But all this was forgotten when Father was arrested. Father and Jawahar were both sentenced to six months' simple imprisonment. Father sent the following message to his comrades after he was sentenced:

"Having served you to the best of my ability while working among you, it is now my high privilege to serve the motherland by going to jail with my only son. I am fully confident that we shall meet again at no distant date as free men. I have only one parting word to say—continue non-violent non-co-operation without a break until Swaraj is attained. Enlist as volunteers in your tens and hundreds and thousands. Let the march of pilgrimage to the only temple of liberty now existing in India, viz., the jail, be kept in an uninterrupted stream—swelling in strength and volume as each day passes. Adieu."

This was the beginning of a new life—a life of uncertainty, of sacrifice, of heart-ache and sorrow. Everything seemed worthwhile when the cause we were fighting for was such a great and noble one. Each one of us hated parting from Father and Jawahar, but we were proud of them for doing their duty and standing by their country in her hour of need.

After their arrest we received frequent visits from the police.

It became quite a habit with them to come every few days and nose around the whole house. Every time they came they attached some piece of furniture or other movable object in lieu of a fine. They were not very particular about what they took and it did not hurt their conscience at all to take away—a carpet worth several thousands along with other things when all they had to realize was five hundred rupees. At first I used to boil with anger and resentment. Later I got used to it.

While Father and Jawahar were in jail, the Congress was held in Ahmedabad. Gandhiji was then out of jail and he asked Mother and Kamala to attend the session. So we decided to go, Mother, Kamala, her little daughter, Indira, and I. Some of our cousins whose husbands were also in jail accompanied us.

We travelled third-class for the first time. It was a novel experience although later we got used to it. The journey was far from comfortable and it was very long. But it was interesting and I for one enjoyed it. It was an education in itself and for the first time I realized how deep-rooted was the faith and affection that the masses had for Gandhiji and other Congress leaders. At every station, no matter how late or how early the hour, large crowds surrounded our compartment. They flooded us with flowers and food and tried to show in a hundred simple ways that they appreciated the sacrifices that the leaders were making to win Swaraj for the people. I marvelled at the faith of the masses, at the great love they showered on us, because they believed we were helping to free them from the foreign yoke. Unquestioningly and unhesitatingly they were willing to leave the shaping of their destinies in the hands of one little man. And this man was Gandhiji.

So after an unforgettable journey we reached Sabarmati Ashram, of which we had heard so much but knew so little. Gandhiji gave us a most affectionate welcome, and after inquiring about Father's and Jawahar's health, he asked someone to show us to our rooms. We stayed in a sort of hostel for students, very bare and unadorned and not too comfortable. We had to sleep in a large room all together and only Mother had a room to herself. It was very cold in December, but we had to get up at 4 a.m. to attend prayers, then bathe, wash our own clothes, spend some time with Bapu and do as we liked for the rest of the day. Having to wake up so early was rather a difficult task for the first few days. But it was worth the trouble, for the prayers held on the banks of the Sabarmati were very beautiful and I did not like to miss them a single day.

The Ashram was composed of several small cottages scattered about. The main central cottage belonged to Bapu. Others were occupied by Mahadeo Desai and nephews of Gandhiji and other workers. Several families shared a cottage. Usually everyone slept on the floor which was not at all to my liking though I soon got used to it. The food we had was very simple, much too simple in fact. It had no 'masalas,' no ingredients to make it tasty, it was simply boiled. All of us found it very difficult to eat it at first. I for one was perpetually hungry and looked forward to going home and having a square meal.

We had to wash our own clothes at the Ashram. It was no joke washing thick khadi. And in those days the saris we wore were terribly coarse. Mother and an elderly cousin of mine were given a young boy to do their washing for them, but the rest of us had to do it ourselves. The first few attempts were none too successful but by the time we were ready to return home, some of our party had become quite adept at washing clothes. I was not one of them.

We stayed in Ahmedabad for a fortnight and then returned home. We had almost the same experience coming back as we had had on our way there.

Living at the Ashram and being able to see quite a lot of Bapu was a grand experience and one that will remain fresh in my memory always. Quite a few people used to come to Bapu and ask him to solve their personal problems. It was hardly fair of them to have done so, and I never understood why Bapu took it upon himself to give them advice on personal problems. If things did not work out as expected, poor Bapu was blamed.

Father and Jawahar had been sentenced to six months' imprisonment the first time. Soon after our return from Ahmedabad, Jawahar was released after serving only three months of his sentence. He did not remain free very long, for in six short weeks he was back in jail. Since then going in and out of jail has become an incurable habit with most of the members of my family.

Life went on thus, day after day and month after month. I studied at home, and apart from paying frequent visits to the jails, we did not travel much. In 1923 all political prisoners were released and it was good to have Father and Jawahar home again and to hear Father's infectious laughter ringing throughout the house that had remained silent so long. Once again there came about some semblance of a quiet normal life at Anand Bhawan.

4.

The world is equal to the child's desire
Who plays with pictures by his nursery fire!
How vast the world by lamplight seems! How small
When memory's eyes look back, remembering all—
                                                —BAUDELAIRE

Jawahar was arrested in Nabha State towards the end of 1923. Soon after his release when he returned home, he developed typhoid and for a month or more was dangerously ill. When he recovered we breathed a little more freely.

There was a break in the usual sojourn to prison and we

were able to see a little more of each other. It was at the conclusion of the Gaya Congress that Father together with C. R. Das conceived the idea of the Swaraj Party. The first meeting of the party was held at Anand Bhawan. C. R. Das became the president and Father was the general secretary.

In June 1925, C. R. Das died and Father became president of the Swaraj Party. C. R. Das was not only a trusted colleague of Father's but a very dear friend and his death was a great shock to Father. Father was busy with the Assembly where as leader of the Opposition and of the Swaraj Party he had his work cut out for him. In March 1926, Father led the walkout of the Swaraj Party from the Assembly at its Delhi session in obedience to the party mandate, which arose out of the Government's attitude over certain reforms. The speech Father gave on this occasion was superb. Often during those days I used to visit him for a week or so in Delhi and attend the Assembly. I was exceedingly proud of Father in his spotless white khadi, looking very dignified and aristocratic. I admired the way he handled difficult problems and the many questions put to him during the session. He was stern and uncompromising when it came to giving in to anything after his party had once come to a decision. Sometimes he took his colleagues to task unmercifully for some error committed or for some weakness that should not have been exhibited! In spite of his rather autocratic behavior, those who knew and understood him loved and admired him greatly. His enemies feared him and preferred to keep out of his way.

I liked attending these Assembly sessions when a heated debate was on. Sometimes when Father gave 'At Homes' or dinners, as Mother was not present, I used to act as hostess for him—and how I enjoyed helping him receive his guests!

My husband's uncle, Kasturbhai Lalbhai, a well-known mill-owner, was also a member of the Assembly in those days and Raja, my husband, used to stay with him sometimes. Raja claims to have met me there once and to have decided that he would marry me! Unfortunately, I do not remember having met him, a point which even now annoys Raja. I am not sorry, however, that he made up his mind to marry me almost eight years before we got married!

Towards the end of 1925 Kamala fell seriously ill. For many years she had been ailing and had caused Jawahar and my parents considerable anxiety. The doctors suggested taking her away to Switzerland for treatment. In March 1926 Jawahar sailed for Europe, taking his wife and his daughter Indira with him. With them also went my sister Swarup and her husband Ranjit. They were going on a vacation which they had planned long ago.

Father had also planned to go to Europe in June of the same year and I was to accompany him. He had had no holiday for many years and with all the strenuous work he had been doing he felt he needed a little rest and change.

Unfortunately, at the last moment he had to cancel his passage owing to a very important case that had been pending and could not be postponed to a later date. He had accepted this case while he was still practicing at the bar. Much as he disliked to reappear in court, he had to stand by his old clients.

After Father had given up practice, many of his old clients continued to come, begging him to make an exception in their case, but he always refused. The exorbitant fees they offered did not move him. Once a client came with a lakh of rupees as fees for a case in which he wanted Father to appear. Scornfully my father looked at it and then, looking at me as I stood nearby, he said, "Well, Beti, do you think it would be right for me to accept this case?" I did not know what to say and hesitated for a few seconds. I knew Father had very little money then and the sum would have come in very handy; but it did not seem right. So I merely said, "No, Father, I don't think you should." He gave my hand a quick clasp as though he was proud of my decision and turning to his old client said, "I'm sorry. You see even my daughter objects." I had a feeling later on that Father had asked me just to see whether I would prove to be the kind of daughter he wanted me to be, or whether I would succumb to temptation and prove unworthy of him.

I had never been away from home without my family nor had I travelled alone. So Father did not know what to do, to let me go alone to Europe or to cancel my passage also. He talked the matter over with me and said I could do as I liked. I hesitated and was torn between two desires. I did not like the idea of going alone, especially as I had so looked forward to travelling with Father; but I had a feeling that if I did not take my chance then, I might never get one in the near future. So I decided to go, and I think it was a wise decision.

Mother was most distressed and annoyed at Father for having allowed me to decide on such a step myself. She thought it highly improper for a young woman to travel all alone to a strange country. She tried to dissuade me from going. I did not wish to hurt her but I wanted very much to go. After a great deal of discussion, I sailed for Europe, unchaperoned for the first time in my life—a little afraid and a little excited at the prospect of the new life before me.

The first few days I was very lonely and unhappy, but I quickly made friends and time passed pleasantly on board the ship. There were some friends aboard who took it upon themselves to act as my guardians, I being alone and unprotected! Every time they saw me speak to a young man—there were quite a few on the boat—they gave me a lecture, saying it was most dangerous to become friendly with strange men. On the stroke of ten I had to go to bed every night. I submitted to this program for a few days but later rebelled. The result was that I had to put up with more sermons and dark looks, which I survived unscathed.

Jawahar was living in Geneva at the time and was to have met me at Brindisi. Having missed his train, he did not arrive. I was overcome with a terrible sense of loneliness and had it not been for some of my new friends who got off the boat with me, I should have been utterly miserable.

42

Jawahar met me at Naples. We did not go straight to Geneva but we visited Rome, Florence and other cities en route. I fell in love with much that I saw. I had read a great deal about Rome, Florence and other towns. The glory of ancient Rome never failed to thrill me. It was during this trip that I saw a lot of Jawahar, whom I found an ideal companion and a most delightful guide. He was no longer the big brother of whom I stood greatly in awe. He was a loved companion and the few days we spent together sight-seeing were very happy indeed.

In Geneva we had a flat. I had never lived in anything so small before and was rather thrilled with it. But after a while I did not like it quite so much and missed the large rooms and spacious grounds of Anand Bhawan. About a week after my arrival Jawahar presented me with a map of Geneva and an English-French Dictionary as well as a book containing bus and tram coupons. I was told that that was all I required to get along by myself and the sooner I started doing things on my own the better it would be for me. I was also told that as Kamala was unwell, I should have to do the house-keeping. Though I did not find it very easy at first, it was good training and I soon got used to it. I knew very little French in those days and the little which I had learned at school was as good as not knowing any at all. I was rather taken aback by my brother's ultimatum but I knew it was no good arguing with him. So I meekly submitted and tried to make the best of a bad job. The very first thing I did was to start learning French from a young and charming Swiss girl who later on became a very dear friend of mine. Our maid, Marguerite, initiated me into the mysteries of house-keeping and we got on well together. Life was not as difficult as I had at first imagined, though a minor crisis would arise now and again.

There was an International Summer School in Geneva and people from all parts of the world seemed to congregate there, especially students who had come on their summer vacations. There were Indians, Chinese, Ceylonese, Americans, French and German and many other nationalities. Jawahar joined it and after some time I too joined it. I made many friends there. The lectures were given by well known statesmen who were there at that time attending the sessions of the League of Nations, by professors from Oxford, Cambridge and other universities and by some famous authors also. The lectures were interesting, but apart from that, they gave us the chance of meeting all types of peoples from all parts of the world.

During week-ends the school organized excursions, and often Jawahar and I accompanied the others when Kamala's health permitted our leaving her. On one of these excursions we had decided to go to a mountain called the Col de Voza. We were a very merry party, mostly Americans and Swiss. Jawahar, a Sindhi student and I were the only Indians. Our Sindhi friend was a bit of a fop, always meticulously dressed and aware of it too. The rest of us put on breeches and pullovers and thick hob-nailed boots, but our friend the Sindhi (he is a high I.C.S. official now somewhere in India!) came dressed in smart tweeds with posh shoes on! We went by train, then by funicular, and then started to climb towards our destination. After a couple of hours of stiff climbing, we were confronted by rain, sleet and snow, and got thoroughly drenched. Our Sindhi friend had had a tough time trying to climb as his shoes kept slipping every now and then, not being equal to the strain of mountaineering. Jawahar, who never went out on excursions unless he was well equipped with bandages, iodine and other necessary articles, suddenly brought out a pair of rope-soled shoes and gave them to our friend. That helped him somewhat out of his difficulties.

After walking for another hour soaked to the skin, we came across a hot and sunny patch of mountainside covered with fresh snow. Though all were very tired, the fresh snow proved too tempting for some of our party including Jawahar. In batches of twos and threes they sat one behind the other and kept sliding down the slope again and again. I was too tired, so I just sat and watched. Jawahar was preparing for yet another slide when one of the students in trying to sit behind

44

him gave a little push and Jawahar started sliding down alone before he was prepared. At the edge of the slope was an enormous precipice and, unable to control himself, Jawahar headed straight for it. We all held our breath and in those few seconds I seemed to die a million times. Jawahar knew he was going nearer and yet nearer the precipice and he tried to keep his presence of mind. He made a super-human effort to turn onto his side, and succeeded in doing so. He landed on some rocky bits jutting out of the snow. That saved him, though his face and arms were badly scratched. It had all happened in a few minutes but I felt terribly weak about the knees for hours afterwards.

After this episode, we went quietly to the hut nearby, where a huge fire was burning, and gathered around it. Our Sindhi friend along with the rest of us put his smart shoes to dry near the fire. After some time when he went to look at his shoes, he found them shrivelled up and unwearable. It caused him much unhappiness, more so as our thick boots had dried up without damage.

Then we had some wholesome food given to us by the old couple who owned the place; and as we could not return that night, we occupied the new chalet belonging to the old couple. The men slept on the floor and two girls shared a bed, as there were not enough beds for all of us. As it was bitterly cold the girl with me, called Molly, suggested that if I held up the bed clothes she would warm the inside with a candle. Nothing daunted, I agreed and held up the covering while Molly passed the candle to and fro warming the bed. Soon we smelled something burning and to our horror discovered a hole in the sheet. We blew out the candle and crept into the bed thankful that we had not burned the hut itself. Next day we started for home rather weary and sore and glad to get back.

Sometimes I accompanied my brother on his visits to Romain Rolland, who lived at Villeneuve not far from Geneva. I also met many other famous authors, musicians and scientists. Those who stand out in my memory are Einstein and Ernst Toller.

The former I did not actually meet, but he was present at a lecture I attended given by Sir J. C. Bose. He sat hidden behind other people on the dais, but no one even knew that he was there till an American student spotted him and passed the news around. Then there was a general uproar and every one clamored to see him. After a great deal of persuasion he came and greeted everybody shyly and seemed most embarrassed at the demonstration of affection and admiration shown him. He remained but a few seconds on the platform and then hurried away somewhere to the background.

I met Toller in Brussels. He was not very striking to look at, but had amazing eyes that seemed to read your innermost thoughts and was very charming to talk to. Often his face would look immeasurably sad and his eyes would have a haunted look about them.

A victim of the Nazi regime, Toller had had to leave his country and seek refuge in other lands. He was a great poet. His two great passions were truth and devotion to the cause of freedom. He was one of the most fearless men I have come across. If he believed in a certain thing and if his conscience told him that it was right, nothing could prevent him from doing it.

Broken and disillusioned, an exile from the land of his birth he committed suicide and thus ended a brilliant career. The world is all the poorer by his death, but neither his works nor Toller himself can die. They will remain immortal.

After a few months in Geneva we went to a hill station called Montana. It was small, almost a village, but very pretty. We stayed there many months and it was there that I first took part in winter sports. I learned to ski and skate and was fascinated by the skiing, at which I spent many delightful hours.

While we were in Montana, Jawahar and I used to take trips every now and again to Paris, Belgium, Germany and sometimes England. I never did take to England, but I loved France and specially Paris. We used to go either for some conference or just for a short pleasure trip. At first Jawahar used to go alone. Later he offered to take me if I could be useful and act as his secretary. I was thrilled at the prospect of going with him but a little dismayed at acting as secretary, for Jawahar is a hard taskmaster and does not stand inefficiency. However, the offer was too tempting and I straight-away borrowed Jawahar's typewriter and set to work on it to equip myself for the future. From then onwards I accompanied him on almost all trips. It was quite an education in itself, but not always as much fun as I had thought it would be. Jawahar never spared me, for he thought hard work was always good for one. According to him, I had never done any before. He said I had had too easy an existence and a little roughing would improve me enormously. I am sure it did.

When Jawahar was not very busy, he would take me round visiting museums, art galleries and the like. Sometimes we trudged along all day. Whenever I felt tired and suggested our taking it easy by doing the rest of our sight-seeing by taxi, Jawahar would consent on condition that we gave up the idea of going to the theatre at night. To him too much luxury all at once was very bad for one. Sullenly I gave in and preferred to tramp rather than miss the theatre that evening. I must admit it was good training and the sort of thing I would never have gone through in India. At times I almost hated my brother for inflicting what I thought were unnecessary hardships on me.

Wherever I went I made many friends, of all nationalities, mostly students and artists. I had been brought up with the utmost freedom and had been taught not to differentiate between girls and boys. In fact, I was very much of a tom-boy myself, and my mother often had to chide me for it. The freedom with which boys and girls mixed was nothing new or strange to me and I never felt shy or awkward with the people I met. I made some very good friends and we never failed to correspond with each other throughout the years until a year after the present war broke out. After that, gradually, one by

47

one, I lost trace of my friends as the Nazi hordes swept over their countries. I often wonder where they are now, whether in concentration camps or fleeing from place to place as helpless refugees. They used to be so full of life, these friends of mine, so unafraid of the future which they thought they were going to mould into a brave new world of peace and plenty. But it was not to be. Their dreams were rudely shattered and who knows if they will ever be recaptured.

The happiest time I spent was in Switzerland and Paris. Often I have wished I could go back to those days when life was carefree and joyous and meet old friends again. But though plans were made again and again they never materialized. And I never went back.

Early in 1927 the League against Imperialism was held in Brussels and Jawahar was asked to attend it as the representative of the Indian National Congress. I accompanied him as usual. People came from all parts of the world, from far off China, Java, Syria, Palestine, Africa, America and a great many other countries. Some of the most inspiring and moving speeches were made by the American and African Negro representatives.

It was here that I met Virendra Chattopadhyaya, Sarojini Naidu's brother, for the first time. He was popularly known as 'Uncle Chatto.' An exile for a great many years from his motherland, having wandered alone from one country to another without a home or financial means, he lived a hand-to-mouth existence. He had not become embittered as many might have done and did do. On the contrary, he always had a smile on his face and a word of good cheer for everybody. He was clever, gentle, charming and one of the most lovable characters I have ever met. I became very fond of him as he did of me, and the more I saw of him the more my respect and admiration for him increased. Even when stark hunger faced him round the corner he never lost courage. Many a time when all he had for his lunch was a couple of apples, he would insist on sharing it with some poor Indian student who was also hard up. When we went to Berlin in October 1927, we met Chatto again and saw a great deal of him. We had all become fond of him and he in turn gave us all his affection. Perhaps it was because after many years he had met some people who gave him the feeling of being one of their family and not an outcast.

The evening we left Berlin, he came to see us off at the station. Hardened though he was to loneliness and a wanderer's existence, he was very upset at bidding us goodby. As he stood on the platform saying goodby to me, his eyes dimmed with tears. "Krishna, I wonder if it is to be *au revoir* or goodby. I hope I shall see you again, or, who knows, I may even come up to the borders of Hindustan to have a glimpse of you." I was deeply moved and almost on the verge of tears, for I had a feeling that I would never see him again. As the train moved out of the station I waved to him till I could see him no longer. I remember the last smile on his lips which quivered though he tried not to show it. And so we parted, leaving him a lonely, desolate figure on the platform—we to our home, comfort and security, and he back to his life of hardship, uncertainty and loneliness. Off and on since then, Jawahar and I heard from Uncle Chatto. And then news stopped coming. There were rumors of all kinds, some that he was alive and in great distress and poverty, others that he had been arrested and shot in Russia. What actually happened nobody knows. Whether he is alive or dead is still a mystery.

There were many other revolutionaries whom we met in Berlin and other cities. I loved to sit and hear stories of their various activities and was filled with deep admiration for their courage. They had sacrificed a great deal and suffered much, and on top of it financial difficulties were a constant problem. Yet they continued to live as best and as cheerfully as they could inspite of the odds against them. All over the world these exiles are scattered—fine men and brave beyond one's imagination and yet how many in our country know of them or, knowing of them, give them even a thought?

Another very lovable and interesting person who stands out

in my memory is Dhan Gopal Mukherji. He was a young Bengali author who had run away from his home in India and after many exciting adventures had reached America, which he had made his home. He had studied at college by working during his spare hours and thus earning his college fees. After leaving college he started writing books. Unfortunately, in India little is known of his writings. His books "The Face of Silence," "Caste and Outcaste" and "My Brother's Face" are some of the best I have read. He also wrote some delightful books for children, such as "Gay Neck," "Kari the Elephant" and many others.

We were in Geneva when one day we received a letter from Dhan Gopal. It was addressed to my brother, but as he was in England at the time, Kamala opened it. Dhan Gopal wanted to meet us. So Kamala wrote back saying Jawahar was away but he was welcome to come any time he liked. Two days later at about five o'clock in the evening the bell rang. It was the maid's day off. So I opened the door and found a young man outside. I asked him what he wanted and he said he had come to see Mrs. and Miss Nehru. I looked at him doubtfully and asked who he was. He said he was Dhan Gopal Mukherji. I almost collapsed, because for some unknown reason both Kamala and I had imagined him to be an oldish man with a beard and long-flowing robes. But here was a very young, good-looking man with a broad American accent and very friendly eyes. Trying to hide my astonishment I let him in and went to inform Kamala. After a few minutes we returned to the living room to find Dhan Gopal on his knees trying to light up the fire that had died out. He got up as we entered and said, "Hullo there—you folks don't mind my making things a little cosier, do you?" He smiled and with that smile he won both Kamala and me over as he did most people. From then onwards, life was one long surprise where Dhan Gopal was concerned. Sometimes he would turn up with flowers or fruits, sometimes with vegetables which he insisted on cooking in the Bengali way, which was not Bengali at all. He would often take me out for walks, and to my horror as soon as he felt warm he would take off his coat and waist coat no matter where he was, bundle it under his arm and continue walking! He always told me that I was much too restless to be an Indian and that I should sit and meditate for half an hour each morning to gain more poise and calm! He had many idiosyncrasies, but he was the most lovable and delightful person I ever met. We corresponded for many years. In 1932 Dhan Gopal came to India for a brief visit. He had lost some of his youthfulness and *joie de vivre*. Life had been rather a disillusionment. He was not doing very well as an author and he was disappointed. Dhan Gopal had married an American woman and had a little son, Gopal, who must now be about twenty-five years old. His wife was much older than he and was principal of a large girls' school in New York. She was an exceedingly nice person, clever and efficient. She was the regular earning member of the family and I think it upset Dhan Gopal very much to live on his wife's earnings. From 1932 onwards Dhan Gopal's letters became more and yet more depressing. Then they stopped and in 1935 we heard he had committed suicide by hanging himself.

Dhan Gopal was a very dear friend of ours. His death came as a great blow to Jawahar, Kamala and me. We lost a most faithful friend and India one of her brilliant but unknown sons.

In the summer of 1927 my father came to Europe. I was very happy about it and so was Jawahar, as Father needed not only a rest but a complete change of surroundings. We feared that something might happen again at the last moment to prevent his coming and that once again he might have to cancel his trip. However, nothing happened and he wrote to say he had booked his passage. In his last letter to me before he sailed, he wrote, "You and Bhai (Jawahar) have both been insisting on my taking a holiday in Europe and at this end Swarup and Ranjit are doing the same and at last I find it possible to get away in the near future. I am a bit tired with the public work that I have been doing for the last seven years and it is disturbing to find at the end of this long period that I have failed to advance the cause of the country in any appreciable way. So I have decided to take a holiday and no longer deny the pleasure of being with all of you." In the same letter, referring to something I had written about the Brussels Conference (the League against Imperialism), Father wrote: "I have received and read with pleasure your account of the Brussels Conference and your impressions of it. You seem to have turned into quite a little politician, but do not think that being a girl will in any way be a handicap to you. Many women have taken as great a part in the uplift of their country as any man has done and some have distinguished themselves much more than men. It is all a question of one's feeling towards one's country and how seriously one applies oneself to the work of uplift. There is no bar of sex—on the contrary a determined woman's influence is much greater than a man can ever sway. So there is every chance for you. You must remember that true patriotism is in your blood and unless you actively suppress it, it is bound to assert itself sooner or later."

He arrived in September 1927. It was a joy to have him with us and he was delighted to be with his children after a year's separation. In contrast to the time I had spent with Jawahar, studying, acting his secretary and being generally useful and helpful all round, I spent the following months with Father in a lazy, luxurious way. I confess I enjoyed it thoroughly, though on the whole I am glad I did not have too much of it.

We went to London together and stayed in a hotel where Father had stayed many, many years ago, when he had taken Jawahar to Harrow. After our arrival I went to the hall porter to ask if there were any letters for us. "What name, please, Miss?" "Nehru," I said. For a few seconds he continued to look in the pigeonholes for letters muttering "Nehru" to himself. Then suddenly he turned around to me and said, "I knew a gentleman called Nehru a great many years ago, Miss. He was a very rich and very fine gentleman and his wife, a lovely lady. Their young son used to go to Harrow. Could you be related to them, Miss?" I was rather thrilled; and beaming at the astonished porter, I told him that my father was the same gentleman who stayed there once and the other slightly bald gentleman was the young lad who used to go to Harrow. The old porter was delighted and was exceptionally attentive to us after this. It was remarkable the way he remembered our name after those many years and I was both surprised and touched by it.

Wherever we stayed with Father we were treated right royally. No sooner did we arrive at a hotel than the manager sent flowers with his compliments. He then came himself to see that we were comfortable. Everyone hovered around us all the time and I, for one, enjoyed this change for a short while.

Once Father was going to London alone and the rest of us were staying on in Paris. He asked me what I would like from London and I told him I had wanted a short leather coat for a very long time. Jawahar had not thought it necessary so I had not been able to get one. Father promised to get it for me but forgot to take my size. When he reached London he went to Selfridge's one day and demanded to see the manager. The manager came and Father quite calmly told him he wanted to buy a leather coat for his daughter. As he did not know the exact size, could the manager kindly arrange to have a few shop girls lined up, about 5 ft. 2 inches tall, so that they could try on the coat and then Father could judge whether it would fit me or not! The manager was rather taken aback at this unusual request. As Father insisted he decided to humor him. Thus Father bought me a lovely coat and seemed quite unconcerned about the method of choosing it. He did not think it either wrong or unusual. When he told us the story Kamala and I were much amused, but Jawahar was furious. He thought it was very wrong of Father to have done such a thing just because he knew he could get away with it.

In November 1927 we were all in Berlin on a short visit. Jawahar wanted to go to Moscow to attend the tenth anniversary celebrations of the Russian Revolution, for which both he and Father had received invitations. I was very eager to go, too, and so was Kamala. At first Father thought it was an unnecessary trip as we had only a week at our disposal to spend in Russia before we returned to Marseilles to catch our boat. Jawahar was keen and so Father gave in. All of us went to Moscow. It was a tiresome and uncomfortable journey and at times Father was quite put out by it.

Moscow looked grim and dull and yet the men and women one met there, dressed in coarse simple clothes, seemed to have something within them—some inner glow that made them interesting and pleasing to look at. They were full of quiet determination and a firm resolve to bear all suffering and sacrifices in order to make their country the greatest and the best in the world.

We stayed at the Grand Hotel. It was a huge place with enormous rooms. All the furniture belonging to the time of the Czars was covered up with thick coarse cloth so that it had nothing of the bourgeois atmosphere about it. It was bitterly cold. When I rang for the maid in the morning and asked for some hot water for a bath, she stared at me in astonishment. By various signs and gestures she explained that I could not have all that water for a bath and who did I think I was anyhow wanting a bath! I could have half a jugful of water to wash my face and with that I and others had to be content, but not so Father. Winter or summer he had to have his daily bath and Russia or no Russia he had no intention of changing his habits. So he insisted on having a hot bath much to the annoyance of the hotel staff.

Amongst others, Father was to meet Chicherin, the foreign minister, a remarkably clever and shrewd man and a great linguist. An appointment was fixed and a young Russian came to inform Father that he could meet Chicherin at 4 a.m. the next morning as the latter was very busy right throughout the night. Father looked at the messenger incredulously as though the latter had taken leave of his senses, and repeated the message. The Russian nodded and said that Father had understood correctly and 4 a.m. was the fixed time! Father was most annoyed and wanted to know what he was supposed to do till 4 a.m.! As he seemed most reluctant to go at that hour, another time was fixed somewhere near the vicinity of 1 a.m.

The celebrations were a grand and spectacular affair. We were told that the march past of the Red Army had been a great sight. We had missed it as we arrived a day late. In the Red Square was Lenin's Tomb where Lenin's body was kept embalmed in a glass case. During certain fixed hours people were allowed to come and offer homage to the memory of Lenin. This they did in the hundreds standing bareheaded in long queues and hushed silence. Outside, two armed soldiers kept guard and inside, too, there were soldiers. We also went and saw the tomb. Lenin looked so life-like that one expected him to get up and speak at any moment.

One day there was a huge state banquet given in honor of all the guests of the Soviet Government. I happened to be seated between two Commissars with long beards and very impressive bearing. They were charming and spoke fluent English and French. The meal was a lengthy affair. I was rather thirsty but there seemed to be nothing to drink. I did not wish to ask the Commissars. So I held my peace, looking round to see if any kind of drink was available. I noticed small glasses near each plate and carafes placed at intervals all along the table. They seemed to contain ordinary water. I stretched out my hand for some but one of the Commissars forestalled me and filled up my tiny glass as well as his own. I saw him gulp it down. So I, being very thirsty, did the same. No sooner had I drunk half the glass in a couple of gulps than I felt I was choking. My throat burned and my eyes smarted with tears. I quietly put down the glass and ate several mouthfuls of the food before me. After what seemed an eternity I felt a little better and then learned that the stuff I had drunk was the famous Russian vodka and not pure water.

We saw many things in Moscow, the only city we visited in Russia. Most churches had been turned into museums, but now and again one still saw an old man or woman crossing himself as he passed a church. There were huge posters all over the place, "Religion is the opium of the people" and so on. How-, ever, the idea of God had not completely disappeared from the minds and hearts of the people.

The one thing that impressed me most was a Russian prison which we saw. I had seen many prisons since 1920 and was eager to see how the Soviet treated their prisoners—political as well as non-political. In the jails in India, armed guards keep watch outside the main gates. Inside, too, the warders carry batons and sometimes other weapons. When we reached the Soviet prison we saw one man in front of the main gate with a gun, walking up and down. Inside, the guards were not armed at all. They had neither guns nor batons. We went right inside. The governor of the prison asked us to pick out any cells we liked to visit. I do not know if this was especially done at that time for the edification of visitors or if it was a normal practice. We chose some cells and were shown round. Most of the prisoners had separate cells. The doors of each cell were left wide open and prisoners came and went as they pleased. Guards kept watch along the corridors, but did not otherwise interfere. Some prisoners were listening to radio sets which they themselves had set up. There were some musicians who were practicing on their instruments. The prisoners had their own orchestra and once a week they had concerts inside the jail. Some men were sitting in their cells composing music, others were out in the yard or workshop, working. They looked more like human beings than most of the prisoners I had seen in Indian jails who have a frightened, haunted look about them and are treated like animals or savages. Though this prison we saw was almost perfect, I do not think all the Soviet prisons could be like this, judging from all that one has read and heard about them.

Another amusing incident happened to me in Moscow. Once I was sitting at a meeting, clad in a simple Dacca sari with no adornment of any kind. Fineries were looked upon with great disfavor in those days. A young Communist girl who had been sitting beside me for some time bent towards me and almost touched the 'kumkum' (red mark) on my forehead and said, "Why do you put that on? I hope it is not a religious sign, for we in Russia do not like religion." I was rather taken aback as I had hardly ever given it a thought myself. I had taken to 'kumkum' as a necessary part of my dress. When this question was thrust at me, I truthfully told the girl, but she seemed reluctant to believe me. "If it isn't a religious sign," she said, "it must be a beauty spot. Do you use it as such?" she asked, "Communists do not believe in these bourgeois methods of enhancing one's looks by unnatural means." I told her that I was not a Communist, but that I might be converted some day; however, I admired the Russians enormously. The girl was somewhat pacified but still looked at me disapprovingly as though I were a lost soul. It was strange how odd one felt in smart clothes in Russia at that time, and how ashamed. The plainest of our saris looked out of place there. Yet I wondered if a strong determination and will to better the lot of common people implied the negation of all aesthetic values—or if I had met one of those intense women!

After a week we returned to Berlin. Our visit had been brief, but it was a vital experience. Many projects were still in their infancy. What struck me most was the determination and the new spirit of hope that moved everyone we met. Such a spirit can surely overcome a mountain of difficulties. I fervently hoped that they would one day succeed in creating a happier society which would better the state of mankind all over the world.

Father found it hard to understand the new Russia and the collectivist idea of the Soviets. His training and background had been different and it was not easy for him to adjust his mind to new ideas and such revolutionary ones at that. Nevertheless, he was glad that he had gone there. The little he saw was really worth seeing. It was a new country in the making and all of us were tremendously impressed. It was a short fleeting visit, but an unforgettable one.

5.

Must we but weep o'er days more blest?
Must we but blush? Our fathers bled.
Earth! render back from out thy breast
A remnant of our Spartan dead!
Of the three hundred grant but three,
To make a new Thermopylæ.

—BYRON

From Moscow we returned to Berlin and then to Paris. After a few weeks we left for Marseilles from where we sailed back home.

Although I had a longing to return home to see my mother, from whom I had never been parted for so long a period before, I felt a little upset and sorrowful the day we were leaving Paris. I had spent many happy days there and had come to love that gay and beautiful city. I had not quite realized, till the time for our departure was close at hand, how compelling and fascinating a charm Paris had. I wondered as our train slowly left the station when I would next be able to visit France's fair capital. Somehow, I had a queer feeling that I would never see it again and that when I did, it would be greatly changed. Little did I then guess that the Paris I loved would some years later be in the hands of the Nazis, bereft of all the laughter, music and art for which it was world famous.

My father had decided to stay on in Europe for a few months longer. Jawahar, Kamala, their daughter Indira and I returned to India in December 1927 via Colombo. The Indian National Congress was being held in Madras that winter. We broke our journey there in order to attend it. Ten days we spent in Madras and then returned to Allahabad.

Back home, among the familiar surroundings which I loved, a strange restlessness came over me. I was far from happy or contented the first few months after our return. Life in Europe had been full of activity. At home I felt at a loose end and did not quite know how to occupy myself apart from reading quite a lot. I was bored and seemed completely at sea, unable to adjust myself to the old routine. During this time I had heard that a Montessori school was to be started in Allahabad. I had always been exceedingly fond of little children and had been interested in the Montessori system, of which I had a fair amount of knowledge. So I decided to try to get a job there. The job was easy enough to get. But I had forgotten that I would have to reckon with my father. During this time my sister and her husband again went to Europe leaving their little daughters, Chandralekha and Nayantara, with Mother. As Mother was very unwell at that time, I had to look after them; and though I was very fond of them it was not an easy task.

Father had just returned from Europe and one day when he was in a particularly good mood, I tactfully brought up the subject. I told him I felt unsettled and wanted some work which would keep me busy at least five or six hours of the day with work that was congenial to me. Father agreed and asked if there was anything I had in mind. He suggested that I should act as a sort of secretary to him or to Jawahar. Though that would have been ideal, I knew it would not work. There would be no fixed hours and the work would not be systematic. I told him that that was not what I had thought of. I told him about the school and said I would like to teach there. At first Father seemed a little incredulous, but when he saw I was really serious, he flatly refused to consider it. He said I would never be happy spending a great deal of time with a lot of infants; if I wanted to try it out, I could go a couple of hours each day merely to kill time. I guessed he had not taken me seriously. So once again taking my courage in both hands (and it did need some courage to tell Father what I wanted to) I gently informed him that I had already applied for the job and had been accepted. I only wanted his permission. I also told him I was not going to do honorary work. I had hardly had my say when the storm broke, as I knew it would. Father did not mind my working, but he wished it to be honorary work. We argued at length about it, but I remained adamant and so did Father. So away went my dreams and my hopes of becoming a working girl. I loved Father too much to defy him, but for the first time I deeply resented his authority. I held my peace and tried to figure out ways and means of getting Father to change his mind, a thing he did not do easily. I tried to enlist Mother's help. She, too, refused, having her own reasons for doing so. She wanted me to get married and to settle down. If I took a job my chances of marrying would become even more remote. I went to Jawahar and to my delight he not only agreed that I should take up work, but that it should be as a paid worker. He promised to persuade Father to give his consent. Jawahar was very pleased at my decision. Greatly relieved, I left the matter in his hands and hoped for the best. Many discussions took place before Father finally gave his consent and then I joined the school. For almost a year and a half I taught there and was thoroughly contented. Later I resigned, as I wanted to take part in politics and could not do both things. Politics is a whole-time job. The Civil Disobedience Movement was on and I was anxious to give all my time to it.

Throughout the year there seemed to be a great deal of activity in all parts of India. People were becoming more and more politically minded and seemed to be moving forward with a new courage and determination. All round, one could sense activity that was slowly coming to life. Something big seemed to be afoot, something no power on earth could stop, and this was particularly noticeable amongst the peasants of the United Provinces where there was a great deal of unrest in those days. The youth movement was also spreading rapidly and in a very short time Youth Leagues were formed all over India. They held conferences and pledged to work for India's independence. They sent their boys and girls into villages where they lived for a given period and worked among the villagers. I was joint secretary, together with a young Bengali student, of our Youth League in Allahabad and Jawahar was our president. My colleague was a fine courageous youth, full of fire and enthusiasm, but after a couple of years he forgot his allegiance to the Congress and changed his views as well as his sphere of work. One lost track of him. Many of my comrades of those days have drifted into different camps, several having become Communists. Meeting them now, I feel I am meeting strangers instead of old colleagues with whom one had worked for a long time, and together with whom one had faced lathi charges and other hardships.

In 1928 the Calcutta Congress was held and my father presided over it. We went in a large party from Allahabad with special coaches attached to the train. In Calcutta, as guests of the Congress, we were taken to a huge house which was decorated with buntings, flowers and National Flags in honor of the president. Outside the gate, little boys in uniform mounted on horses kept guard. They were a smart lot and very obliging. Whenever my father left the house in his car, he was escorted right royally, first by a batch of young boys on horses sitting very straight and upright and seemingly very conscious of themselves, then by a pilot car with the G.O.C. of the volunteers, Subhas Bose, standing up in it resplendent in his uniform. Then followed my father's car. It was all very spectacular. After a time all this paraphernalia rather got on Father's nerves and he asked those in charge to allow him to proceed back and forth unescorted as he did not think his life was in any danger.

It was during this session that Jawahar's and Father's differences of opinion came to a head. Often they had had arguments and had disagreed. But it had never been to such an extent as now. Father was eager to get the All Parties' Conference to support Dominion status, as they were not willing to give their support to complete independence. Jawahar would not agree to this compromise. The mental conflict between father and son continued and the atmosphere at home as well as outside became more and more tense. In the open session the resolution for Dominion status was passed, but Jawahar opposed it.

The following year Jawahar was elected the president of the Congress which was held at Lahore. Never before in the history of the Congress and seldom in the history of similar organizations of the world had presidentship been handed over from father to son. For Father, it was a grand occasion. Proudly and happily he handed over charge to Jawahar, the heir not only to his worldly possessions, but also in the political field to the 'gadi' of presidentship, the highest honor our country could confer upon one of her sons.

This Congress session was memorable in more ways than one. On a bitterly cold morning in December thousands upon thousands of people assembled on the banks of the Ravi and pledged themselves to complete independence. With that resolution began a new dawn in the history of our country. Men, women, and children had assembled regardless of the biting cold. There, under a clear blue sky, they stood and took the Independence Pledge solemnly and with deep feeling. Jawahar read out the pledge and the rest of the crowd repeated it.

Thus our country pledged itself to freedom. And though a few of her sons have deserted her since that winter of 1929, thousands upon thousands have kept their word and have continued to suffer and strive for the achievement of Swaraj without which India can have no peace.

We returned to Allahabad as soon as the session was over, but the future did not look bright. It was obvious that much hardship, suffering and strife lay ahead. But somehow it did not make one feel down-hearted. On the contrary one felt elated and courageous enough to face all that the future had in store, without flinching.

Some months before the Congress session, Father gave away our old home as a gift to the nation. He had long desired to do so and he felt all the happier for it. We went to live in the new house he had built especially for Jawahar and his family. It was lovely and Father was very proud of it. While in Europe I had spent many hours shopping with Father, buying electrical and other fittings for the new house. Father never tired of these excursions and the delight he took in them was a pleasure to see.

The new house had to be named Anand Bhawan as father could not conceive of living anywhere else but in Anand Bhawan. The old house was renamed Swaraj Bhawan, and still is partly used as a Congress Hospital and partly as offices of the All-India Congress Committee, except when it is locked up and sealed by the police, which it is not infrequently.

On the 12th of March 1930 Gandhiji started on his famous march to Dandi, to break the salt laws with a few chosen disciples. A surging sea of humanity followed him and the whole of India watched this little man wage a novel war of non-violence to win for them freedom and justice, that they had been denied so long. Each town and village also joined in to defy the salt laws, as a protest against the hated salt monopoly of the Government. In Allahabad we had an enormous procession and a vast meeting where Jawahar was the first to make some contraband salt.

Gandhiji was not arrested at Dandi as expected. He was allowed to go to the next village, where at the dead of night he was arrested. It is strange, indeed, how even a powerful Government must resort to a 'thief in the night' method for fear of rousing the sleeping tempers of a people they believe they can crush by repression.

Jawahar was arrested soon afterwards, and suddenly every town and village seemed to spring into action. Arrests, firings, lathi charges and a reign of terror commenced on the determined, non-violent masses. The people stood up for their honor and dignity to defend their precious rights and bravely

bore the brunt of savage attack on their person. Having resigned my job at the Montessori School, I joined as a volunteer
and spent most of my time picketing foreign cloth shops, drill-
ing, organizing processions and doing such other work as was
allotted to me by the Congress authorities. Father did not like
the idea of Kamala, my sister, and I knocking about all day in
the scorching sun. He refused to remonstrate with us and he
never forced any of us to give up the work we were doing. He
was not keeping good health and wanted his children near
him. Jawahar was in jail and Father did not want any of us to
court arrest. His state of health did not prevent him from
working and directing the movement, but the strain of working from morning till night with almost no rest at all was too
great for him. The doctors advised him to take rest. But the
Government forestalled the doctors and arrested him on the
30th of June 1930. Thus, instead of going to a hill station, he
merely crossed the Ganges and entered Naini Prison.

During the ten weeks Father spent in prison his health steadily deteriorated. It was only when he was a mere shadow of
his former self that the British Government thought it fit to
release him. Soon after he came out, all of us went to Mussoorie where the mountain air and homely comforts helped to
bring back some strength to his tired, ailing body. Jawahar
too, had been released in the meantime and stayed in Allahabad. He was able to visit us from time to time and this was a
great help and solace to Father.

But Jawahar was not to be allowed his freedom for any
length of time, and rumors of his impending arrest began to
spread. This made Father decide on returning to Allahabad as
soon as possible, much against the doctor's advice. So on the
18th of October all of us left Mussoorie. Jawahar and Kamala
came to meet us at the station, but, the train being late, Jawahar could not stay with us. He had to leave in order to attend
a public meeting. Hundreds and thousands of peasants had
come from the surrounding villages to attend it. After the
meeting, as Kamala and Jawahar were returning home, their

car was stopped in sight of our house and Jawahar was arrested and taken away once again to Naini Prison without being allowed a word of farewell to his ailing father, who waited in vain for his return.

Jawahar's arrest, though expected, was a rude shock to Father. He had hoped he would get some time with Jawahar to talk over certain political as well as family matters, but it was not to be. For a while Father sat with his head bowed with grief, but his lion heart would not submit to any weakness for long. So, raising his white head, he announced that he was going to start work and had no intention of allowing doctors to treat him as an invalid any longer. It was amazing how through sheer will-power he seemed to suppress the fatal disease that had taken hold of him. But it was only for a short time. Nothing daunted, Father set to work with renewed energy and set the Civil Disobedience Movement going again with a greater momentum. Gradually his health became worse and worse. He was persuaded by Jawahar to take rest and go on a short sea trip. I was to accompany him but when we got to Calcutta he seemed to feel weaker and our trip was cancelled. I stayed with Father in a suburb of Calcutta for some weeks, and they were heart-breaking weeks. Father seemed to sense that he would not recover and there was nothing one could do about it. He was not gloomy, on the contrary he was always making fun of his illness, knowing full well that it was a matter of a few months here or there. His courage was superb to the end.

One day news came that Kamala was arrested. It greatly distressed Father, as she was far from well, and he wanted to leave for Allahabad at once. But the doctors persuaded him to stay on for a bit. He sent me back to Allahabad immediately and himself followed with the rest of the family after a few days. An amusing episode took place soon after my return from Calcutta. Many of my friends and colleagues were being arrested almost daily and their trials were held in jail. Those of us who wanted to attend the trials had to get special permission from the District Magistrate, a most annoying and bumptious person. One day I went to him to get permission, as a whole batch of Youth Leaguers were being tried that afternoon. The sight of me seemed to make him see red. "What, you here again? Why can't you people mind your own business and let me continue with mine?" I calmly replied that it was my business to attend the trial of certain Youth Leaguers as I was the secretary of the Youth League. At first he refused to give me permission. I told him I would wait until he did even if I had to wait all day. This exasperated him and he wrote out the permission slip. Handing it over, he said, "Now for heaven's sake stop coming here. You people are driving me crazy."

I went to the trial. I little guessed that our friend the District Magistrate would play the dirty trick on me which he did. As I said *au revoir* to my comrades and prepared to leave with a cousin of mine we were both confronted with an arrest warrant for having been members of an unlawful assembly a week previously. We were rather taken aback but there was nothing we could do about it. My cousin Shyam Kumari took no active part in politics. She was a lawyer and had merely come to attend the trial from a professional point of view. Being a Nehru was just sufficient evidence to be 'condemned.' We were sentenced to one month's imprisonment or Rs. 100 fine.

I was sorry for one reason alone. My father was very ill and had repeatedly told me that he hoped I would not go to jail just then. I did not want him to think that I had deliberately done so, contrary to his wishes, and yet how could I explain? It was winter and our prison cell was cold and filthy, with vermin crawling all over the place. Shyam Kumari and I tried to amuse ourselves for a while and then lapsed into silence. I was terribly unhappy thinking of Father and hoping he would understand. At last I fell asleep and woke up hours later to hear voices, clanging of chains and opening of gates. The voices and lights came nearer and we saw them coming towards us. The door of our cell opened and the matron, the jailor and a couple of warders entered. The matron told us that we had been released as our fine had been paid. I could hardly believe this as I knew Father would on no account pay a fine. However, as we were released we tied up our bedding and went out. In the office we found a lawyer friend awaiting to escort us home. We asked him who had paid our fines, but he said he could not tell us. It wasn't my father or my cousin's father but a friend who wished to remain anonymous. It was past midnight when we were released and we had spent just about twelve hours in jail.

I reached home and found everything in darkness, as no one expected me or knew of my release. Only Mother was awake, reading the *Ramayana*. Early next morning I went to Father's room. He was even more surprised than Mother had been at my reappearance. He was pleased to see me, but very annoyed at the fines having been paid. In the morning papers I read a statement he had issued after my arrest the previous day. Friends had come to him asking if they could pay my fine if he himself would not do so. Naturally, Father was furious and had said that he would be deeply hurt if any one paid it up, as it was a matter of principle not to do so and it would be a most unfriendly and unwelcome act if anyone did so. Nevertheless, as Father was so very ill, someone had decided to take the blame if necessary, and many years later we discovered who it was.

Soon after I came out of prison, I went on a small tour on behalf of the Youth League to the neighboring villages, and on my return I found a note for me from Jawahar enclosed in father's letter. It said, "I understand that you are getting caskets and addresses. What exploits are they meant to celebrate? Surely a few hours in jail do not deserve an epic. Anyway, don't get a swelled head, or perhaps it is better to have a swelled head than no head at all."

Father's health grew worse and worse, though he thought he was better. We had always associated health and strength with him and it hurt one unbearably to see him a little bent,

67

looking very weak and ill and his face slightly swollen. At last he was confined to bed. Even then I did not realize that he was so close to death. Somehow, it just did not seem possible that death could take him away from us. He had always fought against odds and won and I was so sure that he would win through again, even though it was death he had to fight. But it was not to be.

6.

Les grandes Ames sont comme des hautes cimes. Le vent les bat, les nuages les enveloppent; mais on y respire mieux et plus fort qu'ailleurs.

—ROMAIN ROLLAND

It was on the 26th of January 1931, Independence Day, that Jawahar and my brother-in-law Ranjit were released unconditionally, as Father's condition was very serious. Twelve years ago it happened and yet the memory of that day is still achingly fresh in my mind's eye. Jawahar arrived at Anand Bhawan and went straight to Father's room. On the threshold he hesitated for a fleeting moment, for Father's greatly changed appearance and swollen face shocked him tremendously. Then he went forward to embrace Father, and father and son clung to each other without speaking. As Jawahar withdrew from Father's embrace and sat down on the bed his eyes were dimmed with tears which he vainly tried to suppress. I do not think I shall ever forget the light that shone in Father's eyes or the joyousness of his expression as he greeted Jawahar. Nor shall I ever forget the agony in Jawahar's eyes as he approached the sick bed of the father he loved so deeply, a father who had been not only a father but the best friend each one of us had ever had.

Those months of Father's illness were not only unhappy and very anxious days for all of us, but were my first experience with sorrow. Although daily Father grew worse, I just could not believe that death was so near at hand. Till then death had kept away from our little family and I had no experience of it at all.

The same day Jawahar was released, many others were also released all over India. Gandhiji was amongst the first and hearing of Father's serious condition he came straight from Yeravda Prison, Poona, to Allahabad. Father was very pleased to see him and Gandhiji's presence seemed to bring him some peace. Many others who had been released also flocked to Anand Bhawan to see Father and perhaps to pay him their last homage. Our house was full of guests but in spite of that, silence and gloom pervaded everywhere, where usually one heard only laughter and saw only happiness. Silently people flitted about the house, some doing some work, and others just aimlessly wandering around. The whole atmosphere was tense and sorrowful.

All of us, Mother, Jawahar, Kamala, Swarup and I hovered around Father all the time. At nights we took turns sleeping near him in case he wanted us. Many a time when I was with him and he wanted a drink of water, he would ask for it very apologetically, not wanting to bother me. I used to feel rotten because he was so considerate and even when in the throes of a fatal illness his thought was for others and never for himself. Day by day we watched him anxiously as his strength ebbed away, but were helpless to prevent it. Till the end he never lost his sense of humor. Often he joked with Gandhiji, or teased Mother about his going ahead of her and waiting to meet her in the next world, but never did he appear afraid of what he knew must be the inevitable end. All his life Father had had to fight battles and most of them he had won. He

69

could not give in, even to death, without a fight and he fought with all his failing strength for many days and nights, striving to live a few years longer, not for the sake of worldly pleasures, but in order to be able to see some good result of the work to which he had dedicated his life. But all his courage was of no avail and death did triumph in the end.

One day, whilst talking to Bapu, Father expressed a wish that the Working Committee of the Congress should be held at Swaraj Bhawan, as most of the members were already present. His last words were: "Decide India's fate in Swaraj Bhawan; decide it in my presence and let me be a party to the final honorable settlement of the fate of my motherland. Let me die, if die I must, in the lap of a free India. Let me sleep my last sleep not in a subject country, but in a free one."

As Father grew worse the doctors thought it advisable to take him to Lucknow for deep X-ray treatment, but Father did not wish to go. He knew better than the doctors that his time had come and he wanted to die in Anand Bhawan, the house he had built with such pride and had loved so much. But the doctors insisted and Gandhiji agreed with them. Too weak to protest, Father was taken to Lucknow by car on the 4th of February 1931. In spite of the long journey he seemed to be a little better the next day, but by the evening he was definitely worse. He could not breathe and was being given oxygen. He was still conscious of everything around him. Towards five o'clock in the evening Dr. Bidhan Roy, who with Dr. Ansari and Dr. Jivraj Mehta and other doctors, was attending on Father, called me into Father's room and asked me to sit behind him and give him support. I did so and the doctors left us. I never found out whether Father had asked for me or the doctors had sent for me on their own. After a few minutes Father seemed to be searching for something and I bent forward and asked him what he wanted. He could hardly speak but with an effort he took my face between his poor swollen hands and with his lips which were unrecognisably swollen too, he kissed my face all over as though in a last farewell. I clenched my teeth and with a superhuman effort tried not to let my tears, which were brimming over, fall on his hands, or let a sound escape me. As I could not control myself I tried to get away from his embrace. Shrewd and sensitive as always, Father must have guessed how I felt; and still holding me he mumbled with great difficulty, "My little daughter must be brave always." I just could not stand this any more and I ran blindly out of his room and sobbed my very heart out. As the evening wore on he became worse. I could not bear to go into his room again, so I sat with some of the others outside his room all night. Worn out with sorrow and fatigue, towards the morning I fell asleep as did my sister, Kamala, and several other relatives who were there. We had hardly slept an hour when my aunt came and woke us up to tell us that Father was no more. Only Jawahar and Mother and the doctors were with him when he passed away.

One by one, we filed into Father's room. He lay on his bed as though asleep, his face calm and peaceful and more majestic than it had been even in his lifetime. My heart refused to believe that the adored father was dead. Jawahar sat behind him, his hand on Father's head as though he were stroking it, his eyes full of tears unshed. My own tears refused to come, for I just could not believe the thing that had happened. Then Gandhiji came into the room and walked up to Father's bed. He stood awhile with bent head and closed eyes as if saying a prayer and bidding farewell while all of us stood around. Then he went up to Mother, who after the first cry had uttered no sound but sat in a corner stricken with overwhelming grief. Gandhiji sat near her and putting his hand on her shoulder said, "Motilalji is not dead; he will live long." Somehow that brought realization to me with a bang and my tears flowed freely.

News of Father's death was flashed across the whole country. In Lucknow itself the news spread like wildfire and hundreds and thousands of people flocked to the Kalakanker

Palace where we were staying for a last 'darshan' of their leader.

The body lay in state buried in flowers. From the early hours of the morning an unending stream of visitors, friends and relatives passed silently through the room, paying their last homage. Gandhiji was a silent witness at the bedside. So was my mother, who looked a forlorn and pathetic figure sitting beside him with whom she had shared a lifetime of honors, happiness and hardships. Standing nearby, worn out and haggard, was Jawahar, who seemed to have aged overnight. Yet he maintained a calm and serene face under the great catastrophe.

Outside the house the crowds kept swelling. On every face grief and sorrow was apparent and hardly an eye was dry. There was a hushed atmosphere everywhere and no words could describe the feeling of loss that all of us felt.

Father was brought back to Allahabad by car, his body draped with the National Flag with Jawahar beside him. Kamala, Swarup and I had left earlier by car, in order to reach home before the others. Huge crowds had gathered outside our house in Lucknow. As we drew near Allahabad, all along the route for miles and miles thousands of people had gathered, their numbers increasing as we got nearer home. About four miles away from Anand Bhawan the crowds were tremendous, and they kept on swelling. As our car slowly made its way between them, murmurs of sympathy came from all around. Seeing that surging mass of people who had come miles and miles to pay their last homage to Father made us break down completely. At last we arrived home, home that would never be the same again, that had lost something vital that could never be recovered. Our entire compound was filled to overflowing. The National Flag which had always flown so proudly was flying at half-mast, as were many other flags all over the city. At last a mighty murmur went up like one great sob from hundreds and thousands of people and slowly the car with Father drove through the big iron gates for the last time.

Everyone had arrived from Lucknow and all was in readiness for the last ceremonies, but the car bringing Gandhiji and Mother had not arrived. It caused considerable anxiety and other cars were sent to find out what had happened. Almost an hour later they arrived and we discovered that they had had an accident. The Lucknow-Allahabad road was not in a very good condition and as our chauffeur had been crying, he did not see a ditch in the middle of the road. Our car was a big Delage and as it hit the ditch it turned over. Miraculously the door had flown open and both Mother and Gandhiji had been thrown out, both unhurt. The driver was slightly injured, but no damage was done to the car.

Soon after Mother arrived home and the ceremonies had been performed, Father was taken in a huge procession to the banks of the Ganges on a bier gorgeously decorated with flowers. To our aching hearts it brought some measure of peace to see how dearly and widely he had been loved, for not one eye in that vast gathering was dry, not one heart but it truly mourned for the one who had been a lion among men. And so we said our last farewell to the beloved father as we saw him being carried away from us, never to come back. That night, as I walked up and down the garden alone, nothing seemed to have changed. The night was clear and the stars as bright and beautiful as ever. Yet for me the whole world seemed to have crashed at my very feet.

Never in the history of Allahabad had a funeral of such impressive and gigantic proportions been witnessed. Nearly a hundred thousand men, women and children had gathered together on the banks of the Ganges at the 'sangam' for the last rites. As far as the eye could see one saw a sea of heads all waiting bare-headed and in silence. Hundreds of peasants had come from adjoining villages to follow the funeral procession.

After the last ceremonies were over, Gandhiji and Pandit Madan Mohan Malaviya addressed the vast gathering. As Bapu rose to speak a murmur went up from thousands of throats like a groan but subsided into a pin drop silence. He said, "Let

73

every man and woman vow here before the last remains of our great hero on the banks of the Jumna and Ganges, that he or she will not rest till the freedom of India is achieved, because this was the cause dear to the heart of Motilalji. It was this for which he gave his life." Gandhiji spoke at some length in very moving terms and tears flowed freely everywhere.

Pandit Madan Mohan Malaviya appealed to the people to bury their differences and to see that the sacrifices of their leader inspired the people to unite and win freedom for India.

For two days the whole nation went into mourning. Voluntary hartals were observed in every town and village, schools and colleges were closed, and all business was at a standstill. Messages of sympathy poured in by hundreds from all over the world.

In a message that Gandhiji gave after Father's death he said, "My position is worse than a widow's. A widow by a faithful life can appropriate the merits of her husband. I can appropriate nothing. What I have lost through Motilalji's death is a loss for ever."

My father was a well built man of average height, though he always gave one the impression of being very tall. He had a fine intellectual face, eyes that seemed to read your innermost thoughts, a magnificent head, and a charming personality. He was already a little grey when I was born; by the time I was fifteen his head was a shock of snow-white hair which suited him enormously. He was rather stern-looking and most people stood in great awe of him, but beneath was a heart soft and understanding and easily won over if one knew how to do it. He loved little children and they in turn adored him. I never came across a child who did not immediately take to him and become attached to him. His own children he loved with a surpassing love, but even to them he seldom made a demonstration of it. As a child, I stood rather in awe of my father, though I loved him dearly. As I grew up and learned to know him better my awe of him disappeared completely. As the years went by we became great friends, and he was the best friend I ever had. Father had a strong overpowering personality and a kingliness which made him stand apart from all others in any gathering in which he was present. To us his children and to many others dependent upon him, he was a tower of strength. And I am afraid we took full advantage of the fact.

Father was never happier than when surrounded by his family, but we were seldom allowed to be just by ourselves. Friends and relatives used to drop in in the evenings, for that was the only leisure time Father had when he could relax and talk to them. All day long and sometimes late into the night he worked. I remember so vividly even now my father at the dinner hour after a tiring day's work. Sitting at the head of the table amongst those he loved, paying attention to each and every one of us in turn, laughing, teasing and joking, he was different from the stern person outsiders thought him to be. He noticed every little thing about us, a new way of dressing, a new style of doing the hair. He had a most uncanny way of guessing what was passing through the other person's mind. Sometimes he praised one of us, though rarely, for he was not given to pampering. I remember too how Mother used to blush with happiness when Father paid her a compliment, or when, relating some old anecdote, he seemed to forget the presence of his children and relived just the past with his wife. Such memories are unforgettable and I cherish them. To me nothing in the world is more beautiful than to see two people with snow-white hair who have gone through life as comrades, whose affection and understanding has deepened with the passing of years and who have tasted of life's joys as well as its sorrows and have remained unscathed.

Father was at his best in the evenings after the day's work was over. He had a couple of hours' respite before he had dinner and then settled down to more work. Round about 6:30 p.m. or so, father's friends would start arriving one by one and soon a couple of dozen were assembled. Chairs and tables were arranged on the lawn and there he would hold his little court daily among his friends and admirers, entertaining them with his brilliant wit, laughter and merriment. At these gatherings Father as usual took the lead and held the others spellbound as he related some old anecdote or recent incident. The others also got their innings now and then.

Few people understood my Father. Those who met him for the first time thought he was very stern and unbending and altogether formidable. He was that at times, but those who knew him well know how utterly lovable he was. He had a tremendous personality and great charm, and no matter what sort of gathering he was in, he was always the centre of attraction. At social functions also he was the favorite, much to the dismay of many a younger man. He was a bit of an autocrat, very imperious and proud with a certain grandeur and magnificence that was bound to command the respect of all who knew him. There was no pettiness about him and no weakness. Strong in mind as well as in body, he was to me something unique. I have travelled a fair amount and met a great many men and women who were splendid in many ways and whom I have greatly admired. But I still have not come across a man like my father with all his noble qualities. Maybe I am prejudiced in his favor because of the great love I bore him and the intense admiration I had for him.

His one fault was his temper. But it was a fault handed down to him from a long line of ancestors and not one of us is immune from it. Perhaps his only weakness was his amazing love for his children. Most people thought he was a cold and a very strict parent, but beneath his somewhat stern exterior was a heart full of immense love for his family. The whole burden of family affairs fell on his shoulders as Jawahar never took much interest in them. We little knew what worries assailed him, for he would never burden us with anything. While he was alive, we lived a happy, care-free life, knowing he was there to guard and protect us. Shielded by his love, we little knew what care and anxiety were. The very thought of him was a comfort. He was a tower of strength and a refuge from all hardships and pettiness of life. After his death all of us felt completely at sea and could not adjust ourselves to an existence without him.

To the country as well, his death was a great calamity, for, at a most critical time in her history she lost one of her greatest fighters and statesmen. Father's resourcefulness was wonderful and at that juncture his guidance would have been of great value. As one of our leaders said while paying tribute to him, "His spirit of self-sacrifice was far greater than that which is given to ordinary man. In our struggle for independence, he delighted to pile sacrifice upon sacrifice and knew no measure for the volume of his sacrifice. The cause of India he made his own and he did not live for anything but the liberation of India. When a free India erects its Pantheon, Motilalji will have a great place near the one occupied by the architect of modern India, Mahatma Gandhi."

7.

Kado gesu men kais o Kohkan ki azmayash hai,
Jahan ham hain vahan daro rasan ki azamayash hai.

—GHALIB

(For the world outside the test is one of beauty and love,
But for us here, the hangman's rope and prison chains.)

After Father's death Jawahar had to go to Delhi for discussions with Gandhiji, who was having interviews with the Viceroy, Lord Irwin. There were many family matters that had to be looked into by Jawahar, but had to be kept pending owing to his absence. In spite of his preoccupation at Delhi, he did not forget that he was the head of our little family. At

77

that time all of us needed his presence badly, especially Mother who was completely broken. As the days slowly dragged on and he was still unable to return home he wrote to me:

"I seem to be hung up here indefinitely though I had hoped to get a clear week in Allahabad to settle our domestic affairs in consultation with the family. So far the whole burden had fallen on Father and all of us were relieved by his loving care and foresight of a host of difficulties. His amazing love for his children enveloped us and protected us and we lived our lives free from the cares and anxieties which most people have to face. The very thought of him was a comfort when the hard facts of life confronted us. We have to do without him now and as every day passes I feel his absence the more and a terrible loneliness takes hold of me. But we are children of our father and have something of his great strength and courage, and whatever the trials and difficulties that may come our way, we shall face them with resolution and with the determination to overcome them."

This letter shows only too plainly how deep was the sorrow Jawahar felt at the loss of Father, a sorrow shared by us all with the same intensity. We felt so utterly lost without him and did not know how to set about things without his guidance and care. On Jawahar's shoulders fell the entire burden of our little family and he bore it bravely and efficiently. Soon he took Father's place and we started to depend on him more and more for every little thing. We still do so.

Jawahar's letter was like a balm to me. It helped to heal my sorrow more than anything else would have done. Though Jawahar does not know it, innumerable times when I have been overcome by despair or have been down-hearted this letter written twelve years ago has given me courage to face life's problems.

The Indian National Congress held its sessions at Karachi that year, and Mother and I accompanied Jawahar and his wife there. Jawahar was not at all fit. He had been unwell in jail just before his release and the strain and shock of Father's illness and death proved too much for what he always calls his "iron constitution." The doctors advised a long holiday and complete rest. So Jawahar, Kamala and Indira went to Ceylon on a three weeks' trip. Jawahar was delighted with Ceylon and all of them were overwhelmed by the kindness and affection shown to them by the people. Jawahar wrote to me from aboard ship on his return journey:

"We have had a welcome everywhere, magnificent and amazing. And as I went from one great crowd to another and passed numberless people waiting for hours by the wayside, I wondered at this miracle and tried to fathom its meaning. I realised there must be something behind it, something obviously more than individual preference. And I felt suddenly that it was the glory of India and her great fight that they were honoring and we were just the poor symbols and embodiments of that glory. There was a time not so long ago when an Indian had to hang his head in shame in foreign countries. But something has happened and that shame seems to be a thing of the past, a painful dream that has passed away. Today it is a proud privilege to be an Indian and especially one who has borne his share in the heat and burden of the fray, and wherever any one of us may go, he or she carries a bit of the glory of the New India."

Jawahar felt then and feels even today that any honor thrust upon him or any show of great affection is not his personal due but merely a gift given to him because he is one of India's fighting sons, one who has given his all to his country and would even give his life if the country demanded it.

In spite of the Gandhi-Irwin pact, the situation in the country remained unchanged. The Government seemed to have no desire to accept the spirit of the pact and the people already roused were not willing to see the fruits of their struggle thrown away.

In the United Provinces there continued to be unrest and dissatisfaction among the peasants, and ordinances were promulgated by the Government in order to deal with the agrarian

79

troubles. The Provincial Conference which was to be held in the United Provinces was banned by Government unless the conference promised not to deal with the agrarian problem. As the conference was meeting expressly for this purpose it seemed ridiculous for it to give in on this issue. But Gandhiji was soon due back from the Round Table Conference and as Jawahar and others wished to meet him, they thought it advisable to postpone the conference. In spite of it they were unable to meet Gandhiji.

In December 1931 Jawahar was arrested at a wayside station a few miles from Allahabad en route to Bombay. Two days later Gandhiji returned to Bombay from England, having attended the Round Table Conference. He had expected to be met by Jawahar on the pier, but instead he was greeted by the news that Jawahar and several other leaders had been arrested and that innumerable ordinances had been promulgated in different provinces. The die was cast and once again the fight began. On January 4, 1932, Gandhiji and Vallabhbhai were arrested and detained without a trial, and within a few weeks the movement was at its height. Many of us who had not taken very active part in the previous movements now threw ourselves with all the strength and enthusiasm at our command into the struggle. My mother, aged and delicate though she was, did not lag behind. She went about addressing meetings both in the towns and adjoining villages. She was a constant source of surprise to us. All her life she had been more or less an invalid, unable to live a normal active life, but suddenly she seemed to have gained strength and great determination from some higher source. She became quite as energetic as we were, sometimes more.

Soon my sister and I, as well as some of our colleagues, were served with a notice that we should refrain from taking part in meetings or processions, and from organizing hartals, for a period of one month. Independence Day was two weeks ahead. So we planned to lie low until then. On the 26th we had one of the largest meetings ever held in our home town. Mother presided and gave a fiery speech, but before the meeting could terminate there was a lathi charge and the meeting had to break up. Many were arrested on the spot, a great many were badly injured. But though we had expected to be arrested, having broken the order served on us, nothing happened and we went home rather disappointed. Next morning however, at 9:30 a.m. a police car arrived with an inspector, and my sister and I were informed that we were under arrest. We got our things together and said goodby to Mother and others and then left for our prison home. It was our first real experience; I had been to jail once before for twelve hours. We had no thoughts for ourselves or our future, only for our frail little mother whom we had left behind all alone in the huge house which had known so much of joy and happiness, but knew only sorrow and loneliness now. It must have been very hard for Mother to watch her children all go to jail, one by one leaving her alone to carry on her work as well as theirs. But though her body was frail, her heart was as proud and strong as that of a lioness; and though she was left terribly alone with just her sister, another very brave old lady, never once did she falter in her resolve to carry on the fight.

And so we drove away from our loved home to the district jail. When we got there, we found many of our women comrades already there, all cheerful and smiling, prepared for anything that might befall them. We were glad to be together. After some formalities like weighing, and so forth, we were taken inside. The prison had no special women's quarters. As a rule women prisoners were kept there only pending trials and then transferred. One yard was kept for them, and there were women of the worst type with all sorts of diseases. Among them we were kept for three weeks before our trial and four days after it; but we were kept in separate cells four of us in each cell. Each morning the Superintendent, an Englishman who had got shell-shocked rather badly during the last war, came on his rounds. We all had to be present for him to see with his own eyes that none were missing. One day a friend of mine and I were rather late in appearing outside our cell. As soon as he saw us he shouted, "Hurry up, hurry up, I can't wait here all day for you. A tennis tournament is on which I must see and I am held up here in this most unpleasant place." I was very annoyed too. So I retorted back, "We find this even more annoying than you do, as everything is so filthy here. And as for missing the tennis tournament, why should you not miss it one day when we are missing it daily?" The Superintendent went almost livid, but fortunately said nothing further.

The first few days were a novel experience and one that none of us can ever forget. Our cells had all sorts of insects crawling around and for several nights we could not sleep for fear that these beastly things might get into our beds. It was an awful feeling to imagine hour after hour that some queer slimy insect might crawl up one's arms or feet at any moment. Once or twice it happened to each of us. Later on we had a general clean up before retiring each night and nothing untoward happened for the rest of our stay there. During the period before our trial we were allowed visitors daily and Mother came to see us every day. At last the morning of our trial dawned and we waited for the appointed hour rather excitedly. Somehow we did not expect to get more than six months each and we were quite prepared for it. The trial took place in the jail and we all sat in a line and were merely mentioned by name as each case was taken up. We refused to take part in the trial. My sister was the first to be named, and when the Magistrate in a very low voice read out the sentence of one year's rigorous imprisonment plus a fine we were all taken aback. Then came my turn and I got the same sentence with no fine. One by one the other girls got sentenced, only two others getting a year. The rest received varying sentences of three to nine months each. After four days, we were transferred one night at 11 p.m., to Lucknow, where we remained for eleven months and a half—a fortnight we got for good conduct.

We arrived at our destination on a very cold winter morning and the grim prison walls towering above us unrelenting and sinister made our hearts sink a little. For the first time we realized what prison life would mean, to be shut out from the outside world for a year. But each and every one of us was determined not to let it cow our spirits; and in spite of many hardships and mental sufferings we held fast to our faith in our cause and the greatness of our leader.

We entered the prison office and had our things examined, then we were led away inside the prison. The matron showed us our barrack and told us what we were expected to do and how we were expected to behave, and so on. Then she left us after informing us that we were free to walk about our yard, but would have to be locked up at 5 p. m. That was a bit of a shock. However, we arranged our beds, which were none too good, and had a wash and some of us decided to have a look around.

It was morning, and the convicts were all out of their cells, washing or doing odd jobs. As we passed them in rather a leisurely manner, some just looked at us curiously, some even gave a friendly smile, but quite a few of the older and more hardened ones looked at us sullenly. One convict whom we later found out to be a very vindictive old hag and who happened to be a wardress looked us up and down with great disdain.

Mondays in jail were parade days. That meant that the Superintendent came on inspection. There was a great commotion from 5 a.m. onwards, cleaning the yards and barracks. By 8 o'clock all the convicts were lined up in very clean-looking uniforms, with their brightly polished iron plates before them.

Our matron was rather perturbed on our first parade day, as she was not sure how we would behave when the Superintendent came to our barrack. All prisoners were supposed to stand up when he arrived, but in some jails the politicals had refused to do so; hence our matron's concern.

However, the first inspection went off beautifully. The

Superintendent was very courteous and asked us if we had any complaints to make or wanted anything. Some of my companions asked for books or for other things. I wanted to study while I was in jail, so I asked if I might have some French and Italian books, some books on shorthand and three dictionaries. Of course, I told the Superintendent, as these were study books, I also wanted a couple of novels thrown in.

I had asked for these books in all seriousness, not realizing that I was a prisoner and we were not allowed more than six books at a time, dictionaries included.

For a moment only, the Superintendent hesitated, then very seriously he replied, "Would it not be better if I asked permission from the authorities to install a small library for you inside the jail? You would have a greater variety to pick and choose from." And while I hesitated to give a reply, I saw a smile lurking in his eyes, so I replied, "That would be lovely if it is not too much trouble for you. You see I do not want to waste my time in here just twisting yarn. So I hope you will let me have the books soon." I did get my precious books after a great deal of deliberation from the authorities and after two long months.

We were allowed only six saris each and a few other garments. These we had to wash ourselves every day and it was no easy task. The khadi was thick and heavy and, soaked in water, it became even heavier and very difficult to handle. But we soon got used to it, as to so many other things in jail. The food we were given was terrible and though we made valiant efforts to eat it we could not do so. It was not only that the food was bad that upset us; it was served up in such a dirty manner that it made one sick at the sight of it. We asked for permission to cook for ourselves and this was granted. We made up batches of fours and sixes. One person in each group did the cooking, one cut the vegetables and others washed the dishes, and so forth. After this arrangement we felt a little happier.

There were ten and sometimes twelve of us in a barrack.

All day we were free to roam around our yard, but at 5 p.m., we were locked up and let out the next morning at six. The hours between were the most difficult to pass. Each one of us wanted to do something different—some wanted to talk, others to read or discuss things and others wanted to sing and make merry in order to forget the hardships they were undergoing. At times we got on each other's nerves terribly, but on the whole we managed to live together fairly amicably.

News from outside was often disturbing and each time we heard something it left us unsettled for many a day. Once we heard that Mother had been badly wounded in a lathi charge. Not having any particulars, my sister and I were almost frantic with worry, and yet we were not allowed to send a telegram or letter as we had both written our fortnightly letter some days ago. It was at such times that one felt helpless, bitter and frustrated.

Interview days were red-letter days for us. Sometimes no one came as most of our family was in jail and only my mother was out. She had to interview my brother, brother-in-law and my sister and me, so very often if she were ill or had some work to do, we had to forego our interview and this was most depressing.

Every fortnight we were weighed, and if by chance anyone had gained a pound or two, it was something awful! The scales were blamed and the vile jail food, and of course the doctor who weighed us never heard the end of it! In fact I do believe the poor man lost several pounds each time he came to our barrack. The Superintendent and the doctor were the only two men allowed in the women's prison and though the most ardent feminists among us denied emphatically that it was good to see a man occasionally, they spent most of the time he was in our yard talking to him and blaming him for everything that went wrong in jail.

So life went on day after day, month after month. Sometimes we were dull, and lonesome for those whom we had left in the world outside. Sometimes we were happy and contented, working, reading or discussing things with one another.

We found all the young girl-convicts quite friendly and some of them were amusing and clever too. They could dance and sing and one of them, an Anglo-Indian, was quite an expert at it. She was a curious creature and must have been very attractive when she was younger. I shall call her Mary, as I do not wish to give her real name. Usually she was kept in a solitary cell, as she was forever getting into mischief. She was full of cunning and was very stubborn. One day when she was out of her cell for a short while, she came up to me and said, "Do you know, Madam, I am related to a great English actress. Yes, I am, though you may not believe it."

"Why did you come to jail, Mary, and why on earth don't you behave so that you can get your remission and go home?"

"Oh, my dear," she said, "as one prisoner to another, I shall tell you a secret. You know, I have been in and out of jail many times. Each time I go out I am pursued by men. They think I am very beautiful and often enough I am mistaken for my famous actress cousin. They annoy me so much that I just have to do something to get back into jail, where I am free from their attentions!"

One night when all was deadly quiet and every one was asleep, the girl next to me woke me up. "Listen," she said, "do you hear anything?"

I listened, and every now and then I heard the jingle of bells, faint in the distance. "What is it?" I asked.

"I do not know," said my friend, "but it gives me a creepy feeling. There was a dancing girl here who was sentenced to death and hanged. Maybe it is her ghost that haunts the prison."

I shivered. I had no desire to see ghosts in prison, or elsewhere, but I pretended not to bother about it. I told my friend not to imagine things and that it was not possible to have ghosts strolling around a prison. Even they, I was sure, would draw the line at that. My friend did not think it at all funny

86

and snubbed me accordingly. The sound became more and more distant and soon we could not hear it at all.

The next night we again woke up to hear the same sound and we did not feel at all happy about it. We lay awake trying to figure out what it could be but were not successful. For three nights this went on, and on the fourth night, the noise came nearer and was much louder. With tense nerves we waited and soon we saw a figure all in black turn round the corner of one of the barracks and the jingling sound came from it. For a few seconds we could not make out what it was; then, like a flash, it dawned on us that it must be a wardress. Our relief was so great that we nearly shouted with joy. The wardress was supposed to go round the whole women's jail every night; but being very lazy, not thinking it necessary to come into the political prisoners' yard, she had kept away from us, and had gone on her other rounds. The jingling sound came from the enormous bunch of keys hanging at her waist.

Next morning we decided to tell the others and have a good laugh at our own expense. As soon as we started our story, we saw the others looking at each other very meaningly. We questioned them and after much persuasion, they told us that each one of them had heard the bells and had come to the same conclusion as we had about the ghost but they had not told us for fear of alarming us.

But every episode in jail was not one over which we could laugh. The treatment meted out to the young girl-convicts made one's blood boil and yet we were powerless to help them. The wardresses were of the worst type and were generally rude and insulting to all the politicals. It was a difficult job keeping one's temper in control when they spoke rudely to us but it was far worse to see and hear them abusing the other convicts for some very petty thing.

The days dragged slowly on. We went through the winter, sharp and bitter as only the north knows, with no doors to keep out the cold and the biting winds, just iron bars which were hardly any protection. Then came a few pleasant days, but all too soon they ended and the summer started with its dust storms and hot winds. This was even more unbearable than the winter days, but we survived.

The welcome rains and winter approached once again. Towards the end of December, my sister and I were released. Some of our comrades had left before us, others had come after us and we had to leave them behind. Even though we looked forward to going home again, we felt a little said at deserting our comrades.

Jail life had not been pleasant; but it had been a great experience, and I, for one, was very glad to have been able to make friends with some of those convicts who were considered a menace to society, but who were far better specimens of humanity than many of the people we come across in our daily life. I was glad to be going home, but it hurt to know that these poor creatures were to be left behind for many long years and when released they would have no home to go to, no shelter, no helping hand to guide them to a new life: nothing except the cunning that they had learned in jail to help them eke out an existence for themselves until, condemned by society and knocked about from pillar to post, they would at last in desperation commit some crime. This they would often do in order to relieve their hunger, driven by necessity. Then, back in jail once more, perhaps for the rest of their lives.

We read so often in the newspapers about young girls being sentenced for some terrible crime, of women who have murdered, of others who have been sentenced again and again, and we shudder to think that such things can happen. Little do we know, living a life of ease and surrounded by the care of those who love us, what temptations our less fortunate sisters are faced with. We are ready and willing always to show a righteous horror when we hear or read of a ghastly crime, but I wonder how we would act if we lived under the same circumstances as those who are forced to do such things.

We were in a juvenile prison and all the convict girls were under twenty-one years of age. It was strange how sensitive, affectionate and understanding most of these girls were whom society considered a menace. They were frank and open hearted if treated with kindness and friendship. And yet these poor girls were condemned to long terms of imprisonment because life had been unkind to them and in a moment of anger they had given way to certain murderous instincts that a great many of us feel but are too civilized to give in to. It made me a little sad to leave these new found friends of mine behind. I felt ashamed of having so many of the good things in life when they had nothing.

I had become very fond of one of the girls, called Bachuli. She was a fair, grey-eyed girl, plump and not quite five feet tall, with hair down to her shoulders, matted and coarse. Yet, in spite of her rough clothes and none too clean an appearance, she made a pretty picture when I saw her for the first time against the grim prison walls trying to learn to crochet. She looked so very young and had such an innocent expression that I wondered why she was in jail, or what great offence this mere child could have committed. When I walked up to her she was humming a song, one of those sad haunting melodies one hears in the mountains of northern India.

"What is your name?" I asked her.

She looked at me suspiciously and asked in her turn very gently and hesitatingly, "Who are you and how did you get in here?"

"I am a prisoner too," I replied and she burst out laughing.

"What are you in for?" she asked again. I told her I was a political prisoner and though she nodded her head wisely, I think she but vaguely understood what it meant. Anyhow she decided I was trying to be friendly, and being satisfied that I was no jail official, she told me her name. Shyly she looked up at me with a very lovely smile and then with a sigh resumed her work.

"Why are you here, Bachuli?" I asked. A pair of large frank eyes looked straight into mine and she said simply, "For murder."

"For murder?" I asked incredulously and she nodded her head to confirm it. I could hardly believe my eyes or ears. This child still in her teens could not possibly have murdered anyone. There must be some mistake.

"Bachuli, why did you have to murder someone?" I asked. "You are so young. Perhaps you did not know what you were doing. It may have been an accident." She raised her head slowly and looked at me again. The laughter had gone from her eyes and in its place came a look of fear and hatred which hardened her usually soft expression.

This is her story:—

"It was my husband I murdered," she said slowly. "He was very cruel to me and beat me and locked me up very often. He also made me starve and though there was always enough to eat in the house, he would take my share away from me and give me very little of it, eating the rest himself or throwing it away. Every now and then he would invent some new way of causing me pain, though I tried hard to please him. He was very good-looking and when I married him I was only fourteen years old, but I liked him and I vowed to the Gods and Goddesses that I would be a good wife to him, serve and obey him, as my mother had told me to, and feed him well. But a few months after our marriage he suddenly started being cruel, and it gave him pleasure to see me being afraid of him. He told me that he teased me because it amused him, and I was terribly afraid.

"For nearly a year I suffered. My husband would not let me go back to my parents, though I begged him to do so. Each day I became more and more unhappy. In spite of all this illtreatment, I tried to make him like me, but nothing I could do would help or please him. One morning he gave me a thrashing because I had not washed a coat of his that he wanted to wear, and after the thrashing he went out, leaving me in agony. Some hours later he returned, dressed in new clothes with a bright red-silk handkerchief around his neck. I was doing some work and did not turn round when he entered. So he called to me,

'Come here, you little idiot, and admire my new clothes. Do I not look handsome in them?'

"I did not reply, but looked at my own clothes, which were dirty and torn.

"'Speak up, can't you?' he shouted. 'Or are you jealous of my new clothes?'

"I still remained quiet. So he came up to me and slapped my face twice, holding my wrist so that it hurt me terribly.

"'Let go of me,' I cried, 'or I shall kill you one of these days. Why should I admire your clothes when you eat all day long and starve me? Why? . . .' and before I could finish or say any more, he took his stick and, abusing and cursing me, he hit me again and again till I nearly fainted, and then he flung me aside. 'Now try and kill me,' he said, and, throwing away his stick, he calmly lay down and soon fell off to sleep.

"After some hours had elapsed I tried to move, but all my body ached and I lay down again. Suddenly I saw my husband fast asleep in a corner. He had taken off his new clothes and hung them up, but the new silk handkerchief was still round his neck. As I looked at him I hated him and all of a sudden I felt I should kill him and be done with him. But how? I looked around and found nothing with which I could hit him. Then my glance fell on the bright, red handkerchief. I do not know how it happened but I was up in no time, tying the handkerchief tighter and tighter round my husband's neck. He woke up at the first pressure, struggled and tried to shout, but I just went on tightening the handkerchief till his eyes nearly came out of their sockets and then he went limp. I let go, and, being utterly exhausted, I fell back in a daze, half expecting my husband to get up and give me another thrashing. But he did not and I lay there beside him unable to move.

"That is how someone found us the next morning. He discovered my husband was dead and sent for the police and ran hither and thither telling all our neighbors. I was still dazed, unable to believe that I had really killed my husband.

"No one came near me till a policeman arrived and I was

taken away to prison. After my trial I was sent to this prison and so here I am. I was too young to be hanged and women do not usually get a death sentence. I got life imprisonment. That is all."

I had listened to this strange tale in silence with my eyes on Bachuli's face. I still could not believe what she had told me, and yet it must be true, as she was in prison.

As though she had told me just a story, Bachuli resumed her work. She was not curious to know what effect her story had had on me. To her it was an incident which in her innocence and simplicity she believed the fates had willed. She submitted to her life in prison as a matter of course, something which could not be averted, and so why worry?

As I looked at her bent head, my heart ached for her. She was so young, still very immature, and looked anything but a criminal. Why had the fates dealt with her so harshly? What was her life going to be? Should not, I pondered, such cases be tried differently and a different punishment given? A life sentence is not a joke. It means twenty years, if not more, behind prison walls, with no knowledge of the outside world, no one but criminals around one, hearing nothing but the coarsest language, seeing nothing but the lowest of God's creatures and learning such cunningness inside the jail as one may not learn outside in a dozen years. Bachuli was fifteen years old. She would be thirty-five when she left the prison. Having spent all her youth in prison, would she remain as sweet and untouched as she was now? Or would she become a hardened criminal who would be shunned by her fellow men and live a life of evil which would inevitably lead her footsteps back to jail?

My thoughts were confused. I stroked Bachuli's head and said, "I hope I see you again, Bachuli. You must work well and get a lot of remission, then you can perhaps get out of the jail quicker."

A bright smile lit up her face. "Oh yes," she said, "they tell me if I give no trouble and work hard I shall get off much sooner and will not have to do my full term. I shall go to my parents and it will be so lovely. My home is in the mountains and I do love them so."

I walked away sadly, hoping that her courage and optimism would never falter through the long years she was to remain in prison. A child of the mountain, this young creature was used to trees, flowers and the fresh air. How would she stand prison life on the plains, the intense heat of the summer? These were the doubts that assailed me, and yet she seemed fairly contented and resigned to her fate. I could not but admire her spirit. I looked round once again and saw her completely engrossed in her work.

A year I spent with little Bachuli in that prison. I often longed for the outside world, but when the day dawned for me to go, I felt unhappy. There would be no bright-eyed Bachuli with me to while away the hours with her talk and mountain ditties, and the thought of leaving her behind made me most miserable. The day dawned which was the last in my prison home and I went round to my comrades bidding them farewell. Suddenly two arms were flung round me and I saw beloved Bachuli, her large eyes filled with tears standing mutely beside me. I embraced her and, making her look straight at me, I said, "You must be brave, Bachuli, and try to be happy. When you come out, you must let me know, and if you want to come to me you can do so."

"You will not forget me in the great world outside?" asked Bachuli. "For they tell me here that no one likes to remember convicts once they are in the great big world." I stroked her head and assured her that it would not be so; and though many years have passed, her memory is still very fresh and will remain thus for a long time.

As I, together with some of my comrades who were also released the same day, walked out of the prison yards and through the prison gates, I sent up a prayer that Bachuli and other young people like her would not spend their lives in jail, but that some kind fate would restore them to their homes and to a life of peace and happiness.

I turned back once to have a last look at the prison with its grim and forbidding wall which held captive dozens of young offenders, all in their teens, and which had been my home for a year. The large gates were slowly closing and through them I still could see the young girls assembled in the yard to bid us farewell. I waved and quickly turned my head away so that my comrades should not see the tears in my eyes; but they did, and laughingly asked me whether it was breaking my heart to leave the jail. They little knew for whom my tears were shed, for they had not learned to know these young convicts as my sister and I had. They had remained aloof from them and could not understand our feelings for them. My tears were not shed because I was leaving jail, for jail had not been a bed of roses for any of us. They were shed because I was leaving behind a few helpless little girls in their teens, girls sentenced to long terms of imprisonment for crimes committed in ignorance and unhappiness, and who, through sheer misunderstanding and cruelty, were made to commit acts which they never would have committed had poverty, neglect and cruelty not been their lot. It was for these little creatures who had been so human, so childlike and affectionate that my heart bled and I was loath to leave them. I was going back home, to loved ones and friends, all waiting to welcome me, while they—what of them, I wondered? I dared not think.

8.

I will make brooches and toys for your delight,
Of bird-song at morning and star-shine at night,
I will make a palace fit for you and me,
Of green days in forests and blue days at sea.

—ROBERT LOUIS STEVENSON

We were not released in Lucknow, but were brought back to Allahabad escorted by the matron of our jail. We returned home after a year to find it deserted. Kamala was ill in Calcutta and Mother was with her. No one knew of our release and we found Anand Bhawan locked up. But news spreads like lightning, and someone, having spotted us on our way from the station, spread the news of our release. Within a couple of hours, our house was full of friends and relatives asking innumerable questions about our jail life. After the quiet life we were leading, this was rather overpowering, and I, for one, was dazed at seeing so many people all at once.

After a few days in Allahabad, Swarup and I went to Calcutta. Kamala was almost well and wanted to return home. So, after spending a week there, we returned to Allahabad together.

Swarup had sent her three little daughters to a boarding school in Poona just before her arrest. The youngest was only three years old, and, not having seen her children for a long time, Swarup was eager to go and see them. The school belonged to some friends and Indira was also a boarder there. While in jail, I had had a bad spell of malaria and was very run down. Mother thought a little change might do me good and suggested my accompanying Swarup to Bombay and

Poona—a suggestion I hailed with delight. We went to Poona direct and after a few days' stay there we came to Bombay, bringing the children with us. In Poona, we had several interviews with Gandhiji at Yeravda. He always greeted us with great affection, and it did us good to spend some time with him whenever permission was granted.

My sister, her children and I were in Bombay for about a week. It was during this week that I met Raja. The first time was at a party. As soon as I entered the room I noticed him. He looked somewhat different from all the others there, with a detached and rather superior air about him that both annoyed and intrigued me. Though one of the party, he seemed not to be of it. He sat silent and aloof, smoking a lovely meerschaum pipe. Apart from our introduction, we did not speak to each other at all. I usually notice people's hands when I meet them for the first time, for to me they always seem to speak and to give an inkling into the person's character. So one of the first things I noticed about Raja were his hands; sensitive and artistic, they seemed to speak volumes for their owner, who was exceptionally quiet. The next time we met was at a picnic at Juhu arranged by Raja and another friend. This time Raja and I talked a great deal, mostly about books and Communism. I promised to send Raja some books from my brother's library. This was the beginning of our friendship and we started to correspond.

In May I went with Swarup to Mussoorie for a couple of months, and on our return, I decided to go to Ahmedabad in August to spend some time with my friend, Bharati Sarabhai, who was due to go to Oxford shortly. I wrote and told Raja about my plans, hoping to meet him either at Ahmedabad or in Bombay. He asked me not to go via Delhi, as I intended doing, but via Bombay. I agreed to do so. As luck would have it, an old friend of our family, in Bombay at the time, heard that I was coming. He and Raja arrived at the station to meet me, each one blissfully unconscious of the other's presence. I saw them both and was rather nervous at the friend's reception of Raja, but when I introduced them to each other, though the friend looked very suspiciously at Raja, he asked no questions.

From that day onwards, I spent most of my time with Raja. We used to go to cinemas and on long drives, but Raja always maintained a distant attitude. Though I knew he must be liking me to spend so many hours with me daily, I did not know if he cared for me, as he hardly gave any indication of his feelings. This was yet one more reason for which I liked him.

I had been used to a fair amount of attention, and I took it for granted that people should like me. This was merely because I did not see any reason for them to dislike me and not because it was my due. Raja's indifference rather piqued me at first and so, maybe, I went out of my way to break the crust which he seemed to build around him. We were together many hours each day. We just talked endlessly and never seemed to be bored with one another.

Just before I left for Ahmedabad one evening, Raja casually said, "When shall we get married, my dear?" Just a simple question put in a simple way by a man whose heart was as simple and pure as a child's.

I was rather taken aback and yet I was very thrilled by this most unusual method of proposing. For a week we had been seeing each other daily and no word of love had been uttered by either of us. I knew Raja liked me, but I did not guess that he was in love. As for me, the more I saw him, the more I liked him. He was so very different from any other man I knew. Yet I was not sure that I loved him, and I told him so. In his cool, quiet manner, Raja assured me that I was in love with him though I might not be aware of it, and would I please say, "Yes." I did not. I told him I would let him know on my return from Ahmedabad.

During the week I was away, Raja wrote to me daily. They were beautiful letters and Raja was most persistent. Being away from him I realized how fond I was of him and how much I wanted to be with him again. I'm afraid my visit to Ahmedabad had to be cut short because I felt I just had to return to Bombay.

So I came back and told Raja that I would marry him. I lived in a dream world, but one morning I came back to reality with a bang. I saw in the papers that Mother was suddenly taken ill. I rang up Raja and decided to leave that night for Allahabad. With a heavy heart I parted from him, not knowing when or how we would meet again.

When I reached Allahabad, I found Mother had been taken to Lucknow for treatment. So I went there.

The only person to whom I had mentioned Raja was my sister and on my return I told her I had promised to marry him. I asked her not to say anything about it since Mother was so ill and Jawahar was in jail. So we kept the secret between ourselves.

Jawahar was unconditionally released, as Mother's condition was serious. After many nerve-racking nights and days, Mother gradually passed the crisis.

It was then that I asked Swarup to tell Jawahar about Raja. It did not seem unnatural for me to have chosen my future husband without consulting my people, as I had always had freedom to do as I pleased. I did not dream of defying or going contrary to the wishes of my mother, brother and sister; but I knew that they would not be unreasonable unless there was a very good reason for it. They knew nothing at all about Raja, but I was sure that they would not withhold their consent, for my happiness came first with them and I was sure that they would all like Raja. I was only afraid they would think we had not known each other long enough which was true. But I did not think long engagements helped one to get to know each other any better.

When Jawahar spoke to me about Raja, he did so in a very characteristic way. With a twinkle in his eye he said, "Well, my dear, I hear you are contemplating marriage. Could you enlighten me somewhat about the young man?" I felt rather embarrassed, but I said I would. Jawahar started asking me what Raja did. I told him he was a barrister and had just started practicing. Then Jawahar asked who Raja's people were and I said I had not the faintest idea. He asked how many brothers and sisters Raja had and I again looked blank. Jawahar was beginning to be exasperated and I trembled and cursed myself for not having asked Raja these very obvious questions. Which college did Raja go to at Oxford? What did he do there? and a dozen other questions were put to me. But I did not know any of the answers. At last Jawahar asked why I called Raja "Raja" when his initials were "G.P." What did they stand for? I was really terrified now, for, though I vaguely remembered that Raja had told me what "G.P." stood for, I just could not recall it. I told my brother rather timidly that I could not remember. Jawahar, now quite upset, said, "This is preposterous." Saying this, he marched out of the room and I was left alone rather crestfallen and unhappy.

I realized that I had been very stupid about it, but somehow all the days I was with Raja, I was so engrossed with him that it had never occurred to me to find out anything about his family or himself. We had discussed many things, but never ourselves. I liked Raja, and nothing else mattered.

That night I wrote to Raja and asked him for the necessary information. He was a little annoyed, but sent the following:

My Credentials

NAME: Gunottam Huthessing.
SCHOOL: National School and Gujarat Vidyapith.
COLLEGE: St. Catherine's, Oxford.
INNS OF COURT: Lincoln's.
DEGREE: B. A. in Politics, Economics and Philosophy.
CLUBS: None—and do not intend joining any.
PROFESSION: Barrister-at-Law. I am keen on it, on everything I do, but that does not mean I may not give it up for something else, maybe politics, in a year or two.

99

HOBBY: Armchair lounging with a pipe. Indulge in the habit of thinking—quite uncommon with most people.

GAMES: Played cricket years ago—do not play anything now.

CHARACTER: Am considered conceited and selfish.

VIEWS ON MARRIAGE: Believe in giving complete freedom to anyone who has any and wishes to preserve it.

REFERENCES: None.

FUTURE PROSPECTS OF A BRILLIANT CAREER: None.

FINANCIAL RESPECTABILITY: Tolerable—can afford to live in moderate comfort—certainly not in great affluence.

FINALLY: This is an application—a presumptuous one, maybe—to ask Miss Krishna Nehru to agree to be married to the above person in October 1933.

Such was the note I received, and it greatly amused me, because I could guess from it how irritated Raja must have been when I wrote and asked for details about himself.

When Mother was slightly better, Jawahar went to Bombay and met Raja. Jawahar saw Gandhiji then and told him about my desire to marry Raja. Gandhiji happened to know Raja's family rather well and said he would like to meet Raja, whom he knew slightly. So Raja went to see him, and was not very happy at the cross-questioning Gandhiji subjected him to. In spite of it, Raja did not back out or falter (I am sure not many a brave man would have withstood it), and accepted Jawahar's invitation to go to Lucknow and meet Mother and the rest of the family. He came after a fortnight or so. Mother was still in hospital, very weak and not out of danger. When she saw Raja she took an instant liking to him and he for her. After that Mother wanted us to get married as soon as possible. I did not want to have the wedding till Mother was well, but she would not hear of any delay. She felt she might not survive very long and wanted to see me happily settled before anything happened to her.

It was on the 20th of October 1933 that Raja and I were married at Anand Bhawan according to the civil marriage rites. It was a simple ceremony and was over in half an hour, a great-contrast to Swarup's wedding celebrations which lasted a week or more. A few friends and relations of ours, as well as Raja's brothers, sister, and uncle, Kasturbhai Lalbhai, were present. Mother was still bedridden, and in Ahmedabad, Raja's mother was lying very ill too. Hence we had decided to have a very quiet wedding.

As Bapu was unable to come to Allahabad, he had suggested that I should be married in Wardha. To that I would not agree, much though I wanted Bapu to be present to give us his blessings. I could not think of getting married anywhere else but in my own home, filled with so many childhood memories and memories of my father who was no longer there. The one flaw at my wedding was his absence, for I missed him sorely. Bapu, however, sent me a letter of blessings and two garlands of yarn spun by himself as a wedding present for Raja and me. He wrote to me in Hindi:

"My dear Krishna,

"You are now going to be reborn, for marriage is a sort of re-birth, is it not? Your sister Swarup came as a bride to Kathiawad but persuaded her husband to go and settle down in her old Province. But there is a great deal of difference between Swarup and you, and I do not think you will try to take Raja away. Besides, Raja is a Gujarati who will not easily leave his homeland. So I hope you will make Gujarat your home, or maybe Bombay. My only wish is that wherever you are, you may be happy and add lustre to the already bright name of your illustrious parents.

"I regret very much I am unable to attend your marriage, so I shall have to content myself with sending you my blessings.

"Your Bapu."

Vallabhbhai was in Nasik Prison when he heard of our engagement. He also sent me a letter of congratulations and blessings. He mentioned the fact that though my brother-in-law Ranjit Pandit had left his homeland and settled in the United Provinces, which was our home, the people of Gujarat would keep me in their Province and not let me go or take Raja with me to settle down in the North. I had no intention of doing so, hence Vallabhbhai's fears were unfounded. But I was happy to know that so many people were willing to welcome me to my new home.

Sarojini Naidu, an old friend of our family, also sent me a letter of congratulation. It was so typical of her, full of poetry and music. She wrote:

"My dear little Betty [an unfortunate pet name that has stuck to me throughout the years],

"How delightful to discover an unsuspected flower of romance to blossom suddenly full-blown and radiant out of the dreariness of our present national life. And what a precious pair of rogues you have been to have kept your secret rêve! I am so happy, my dear little one, in your new-found happiness. Indeed I am doubly and trebly happy because I know what a consolation it will be for dear little Mammaji [that is what Mrs. Naidu called my mother] on her sick bed to have the last desire of her heart fulfilled and to see her baby become a bride. I know too, how Papaji [Father] would have blessed and approved your choice, hiding his deep emotion under some characteristic jest and laughter. He too had this desire in his royal old heart and spoke of it now and then.

"I have had a longer acquaintance with your Raja than you. I can give you many thumbnail sketches of him in various phases. Of him lying in a boat in May week on the river at Oxford making witty comments on the tribes of priests and prophets. Of him in London with flowing tie and a pipe in his mouth haunting the Café Royal and being the complete Bohemian. But my last impression of him was at the Victoria Terminus looking selfconscious and out of place on the edge of a Khaddar-clad crowd bidding farewell to Jawahar, and everyone wondering who he was in that assembly. I wondered a little too, and though he walked down the platform with me, he never even by the flickering of an eyelash belied his intimate concern and about-to-be-intimate relationship with the brother of his choice bride!

"I see that Swarup and Kamala are here to get together a hurried trousseau for you, and are complaining of the limited choice that shudh [pure] Khadi offers for bridal raiment. But why should that bother you, who move clothed in delight and dreams and are adorned with the jewels of your own youth and romance and adventure?

"I pray that you will together make of your marriage a beautiful and enduring comradeship, based not only on mutual affection but on mutual understanding, faith and common interests in the daily plans and problems of life.

"You are bringing as your share in that comradeship some wonderful personal gifts, enhanced by all the richness and nobility of tradition that belong to your family, as the integral part of the existing traditions, ideals and achievements which are an example and an inspiration to the nation . . . and therefore, your marriage is not only a private affair to be restricted to your family and friends. The nation too has part and lot in it, since you are Motilal Nehru's daughter and the beloved Jawahar's sister.

"But you are also my little sister and so I send you, Little Bride, all my most loving benedictions and rejoice with you that you have found your mate and the friend and companion of your youth."

This letter, as well as countless others that I received wishing me luck and happiness, touched me deeply, and I hoped I would make a success of the new life ahead.

A few days after the wedding, I left my old home for a new one, not without many pangs. I hated leaving Mother, who was still bedridden, and the rest of my family. I was a little afraid of the future, of the new life ahead of me; but each time I looked at Raja, so devoted and loving, I felt reassured.

The evening we left for Ahmedabad, all my relatives and friends and almost the whole of my home town turned out to see us off. I felt more miserable at that moment than ever before. Everyone embraced me tearfully, but I kept up my courage. Last of all, as the train whistle blew and I clung to Jawahar, he whispered, "Be happy, darling," and those three little words let loose the tears I tried so hard to check. The parting with Mother had been heart-breaking, but for her sake I had tried not to break down. Now as the train slowly moved away I felt like jumping out and returning home to my people. The die was cast and there was no going back.

As we approached Ahmedabad, Raja's home, he spoke to me about each member of his family for the first time. He was very impartial and gave me a very good picture of them and the life before me. He told me about the difficulties I might have to encounter, also how much he disliked my having to leave my old home. He said he felt as if he were uprooting a young tree that had been planted in a certain soil where it had grown and blossomed. Now it was to be replanted elsewhere and many doubts assailed him. Would the tree benefit by this uprooting and become more beautiful and fruitful, or would it wither away in strange surroundings? Such questions worried Raja as he neared his home, and he almost seemed to regret having married me!

We reached Ahmedabad in the early hours of the morning and were received at the station by his family and friends. After a few days in Ahmedabad we shifted to Bombay. And so the new life began.

In his youth Raja had boycotted the Government school and joined the National Vidyapith. Later, in England, he dabbled in politics as most students do. On his return, he decided to keep out of active politics till he got settled at the Bombay bar. For some time he carried on with his work, but, being always very politically minded, he found it increasingly difficult to remain a distant spectator. Gradually he succumbed to politics. I could see Raja was not happy with his work. He was eager to do his bit for his country, and if need be, to give up everything he possessed and held dear, for the cause of freedom. No personal ambitions or gains have ever marred Raja's political career so far and I am sure they never will. He has ever been willing to remain a silent worker in the background and work unnoticed. He has done so steadily and unwaveringly these many years, in spite of many disillusionments.

Raja is the sort of person, no matter how old he is, who will always retain his childlike simplicity and faith in certain ideals. He is honest and open-hearted, and has immense faith in the ultimate goodness of his fellow beings. He has a very high code of conduct for himself, but does not condemn others who have different values. Such people, idealists at heart, suffer a great deal when disillusionment comes.

Many people have the impression that he is snobbish and conceited. This is hardly correct. His greatest fault, if a fault it can be called, is his over-sensitiveness. Early in life he learned to be reserved, as he was different from others and easily misunderstood. This reserve of his is usually mistaken for conceit. Those who know him well cannot help but be fond of him, not for his virtues (which are quite a few), but for the very faults and weaknesses that make him so human.

9.

Travellers, we're fabric of the road we go;
We settle, but like feathers on time's flow.

—CECIL DAY LEWIS

Since 1920 life had been one of constant change and uncertainty and I never knew what was going to happen next. At first I found it exciting, but when the constant uncertainty continued day after day and year after year, it sometimes became nerve-racking. In contrast, my early married life was very

peaceful and I hoped it would continue thus with few up-
heavals if any. But I was hoping for the unattainable.

Life was not altogether easy the first few months. Ahmedabad, a great industrial centre with all the contradictions arising
out of the impact of industrial revolution on ancient traditions,
seemed a different world of whose existence I was not even
aware. Everything appeared different from the world I belonged to—one's outlook on life, customs, manners and way of
living. Though everybody I met in my husband's home was
very kind, I felt at times lonely and completely at sea. Had
my affection for Raja not been as deep and intense as it was,
I would have found the new life very difficult. Raja's love and
understanding in my moments of despair and the consideration
shown by his family pulled me through at that critical time
and have done so always. I may have failed Raja many a time
but he has never failed me.

A few months after I was married I had a letter from Jawahar which helped me in the process of adjustment. He wrote,
"In your new experience of married life you will have to view
life from a different angle and gain wisdom thereby. But wisdom comes often at the cost of so much, so many years that
slip by and do not return. Those who have had the advantage
of prison experience know at least the value of patience, and
if they have profited by their experience they have learned
adaptability, and that is a great thing. I hope you will soon
settle down and may you always be very happy, little sister."

Strange though it may seem, food was my greatest problem
during the first months of married life. I had never been very
particular about what I ate but I liked meat and fish as most
Kashmiris do. In Ahmedabad I found everyone a strict vegetarian; no meat, no fish, no eggs, nor was there any likelihood
of going to a hotel or restaurant and getting some, as such
things were just not done. I liked Gujarati food but did not
feel satisfied eating only vegetables. For three months I was a
vegetarian, and throughout those months I was more or less
famished. Later I trained myself not to depend so much on

meat and now I can willingly do without it for long stretches at a time.

Raja's family is one of the leading business families of Ahmedabad. His father died many years ago when the children were still very young. His mother then took charge of the business and looked after it successfully in spite of tremendous odds. For many years she carried on till her sons grew up to shoulder the task. During all those difficult days she did not neglect her children but bestowed all her love and care on them and ministered to their smallest needs. Like all business people, Raja's people are reserved, quiet and a little aloof, never showing their emotions to others. At first I could not understand this and often mistook their reserve for lack of affection.

Raja belongs to a joint family but his people rarely interfere in the life each member wishes to lead. They are, however, a closely knit family and attached to each other, not only because of business but by ties of deep affection. The business community of Ahmedabad is narrow, conservative and self-centered and demands conformity to its values, which are often an irritating and unnecessary interference with the private life of an individual, more so when the individual is a member of a joint family. Hence the process of adjustment for us was difficult and long.

The joint families of the past no doubt served a useful purpose and fitted in with the social structure of that age. But that structure is rapidly crumbling now and could not survive in its old form. There seemed to be a constant struggle all over India. The individual asserted his right to his own way of living, while the joint family demanded a more unified pattern. Naturally, between these two, the hold of the family became less and less. It came in the way not only of individual life but also of national life, and could not fit in with the forces that move the world today. I believe that the joint family has to fade away gradually, but India being such a huge country with deep roots in the past, it will take some time.

The family as a unit, however, is important, especially the

smaller one. Living as we did at Anand Bhawan—my parents, Jawahar and his family, my sister and I—we made up such a unit. But there never were any hard and fast rules by which any of us were tied down to the rest. We lived together in one house but led our own individual lives, rarely if ever clashing with one another. No bonds held us together, except bonds of affection which are stronger than anything else could be. The economic bonds that tie up persons in a joint family tend to become real bonds sooner or later, suppressing the individual and preventing his growth and development.

Such views of mine naturally came into conflict with those of Raja's family and sometimes of Raja himself. We discovered that there were many matters on which we could not see eye to eye and our views sometimes clashed. The patience and understanding he gave then and throughout these many years have been something grand and unique. That helped me over the first few months which are always the most difficult.

For some months after our marriage, we lived with Raja's family. Later we had a flat of our own. It was small but ultra-modern and I loved it. I had very little experience of house-keeping and found it rather puzzling and at times difficult. On the whole, however, it was fun to run a home of one's own. Having lived a great part of my life in a large house with lavish arrangements, it was quite a novel experience to live in a flat and in a simpler style.

I found the days a little lonely while my husband was at work. I did not know very many people in Bombay and those I did know, apart from Raja's friends, were mostly my father's old friends and their families. Being quick to make friends, it was not long before I made many acquaintances and quite a few friends. Life was happy and contented.

In the winter of 1934 Jawahar was once again in prison, as he usually is during the best part of every year. We had not seen him for many months so when Kamala wrote to me asking if Raja and I would like to see Jawahar, we eagerly took the suggestion. An interview was arranged and we decided to meet

Kamala and accompany her to Dehra Dun Jail. On the appointed day we arrived at the jail gates and after waiting half an hour or so we were taken to Jawahar's cell. It is customary to have interviews in the jail office, but Jawahar's cell being in an outer block we were permitted to go there. Raja had never been in the vicinity of a jail before. The Dehra Dun jail is not half as formidable as some other jails I have known, but to one who has never been near an Indian prison, even the Dehra Dun jail seemed a grim place. We sat in Jawahar's cell, which was bare and scantily furnished with an iron bed, a table and a chair. Some books were scattered about and in one corner there was a spinning wheel. It was a dull, gloomy day, very cold and windy, and the cell looked dreary and cheerless. Though Jawahar greeted us with his usual bright smile, he looked thin and unwell. Kamala and I were used to such visits and to seeing our dear ones under varying conditions. To Raja it was all very new and he was rather staggered by the whole place. Throughout the interview he sat rather quietly while Kamala and I did all the talking. When we returned home, he went straight to his room without saying a word to anyone. Some time later when he did not return I went to see what had happened. I found him lying on his bed feeling and looking utterly miserable.

Since then Raja has had many interviews with Jawahar in jail but it still makes him a little sad and depressed each time he visits a prison. Seeing dear ones behind prison bars year in and year out is not pleasant. It inevitably leaves one a little sad and sometimes a little hungry for the companionship of those we may not meet. And yet it does not make us feel helpless or dejected but only more determined to carry on our struggle.

As I write this Raja is himself in jail with thousands of comrades, and we have not seen each other for over a year. When I am overcome by loneliness and longing for Raja and he guesses it from the tone of my letters, he chides me for it and always makes me a little ashamed of showing my weakness.

For some years Raja avoided taking an active part in politics but events moved so rapidly and in such a manner that he found it increasingly difficult to keep out of public life and gradually he succumbed. Many people think I influenced him in this direction and made him give up the bar, but they are wholly mistaken. I knew only too well what politics meant— uncertainty, change, prison and long separations. I had had thirteen years of it and did not wish to lose my newly acquired contentment and peacefulness. I did not wish to take active part in politics. My sons were very young. I had seen how Jawahar's and Swarup's children had suffered from infancy from having no family life, no settled home or routine. Yet I could not remain untouched by the happenings around me. So I did the little I could. But Raja longed to throw himself into the struggle wholeheartedly and I did not think it right to attempt to hold him back. Once again, after a brief spell of happiness, I prepared myself for the usual separations caused by arrests and imprisonments.

We lived in Bombay and I loved this big city. Allahabad was very dear to me but only because it was my home and for no other reason. I love a big city, maybe because I spent half my life in a small town. I liked Bombay because of the warmth and friendship it offered—because there is always an air of expectancy about it which is intriguing. The sea was something new to me and I was fascinated by it. All I knew of the sea was what I had seen of it on my way to Europe. I had never lived in close proximity to it for a long time. But in Bombay I had my fill of it and was never tired of watching the waves tumbling over each other or dashing angrily against the rocks.

As the days hung heavily on my hands I took up some social work and joined various women's organizations. We worked in the slums and I found it interesting, but it was very depressing to see so much poverty and misery and yet not be able to do much to relieve it.

In January 1935 Mother came to visit us. Jawahar was in jail and Kamala was undergoing treatment in Calcutta. Bapu had been asking Mother to come to Wardha for a short visit and she decided to go there, as she was all alone in Allahabad. From Wardha she came to Bombay. It was her first visit to my new home and I was very happy to have her. She intended staying just a month but unfortunately after about three weeks she had an attack of paralysis and was terribly ill for a couple of months. My sister and aunt came to Bombay and we spent many anxious days and nights while Mother hovered between life and death.

During this time when Mother was convalescing our son Harsha was born, on the 1st February 1935. Mother was over-joyed. He was her first grandson; my brother and sister both had daughters.

Slowly Mother recovered from her illness but it was merely the beginning of the end. She was never her old self again.

In April 1935 Kamala, who had been ill for some time, be-came worse. The doctors advised her to go to Switzerland as soon as she could travel. At that time she was in a sanatorium in Bhowali, a small hill station in the United Provinces. Raja and I decided to go to see her and be with her for some time. So we took our two-months-old baby and went to Bhowali. We spent a month with her before she left. Little did we real-ize then that we were never going to see her again. Less than a year later Kamala died.

Four days after the news of her death, our son Ajit was born. His birth would normally have been an occasion for great happiness, but Kamala's death threw a gloom over our lives and our hearts were too heavy to rejoice at the birth of our baby. Yet I think his very presence helped somewhat to lessen the blow and alleviate our grief.

IO.

The fairest things have fleetest end,
Their scent survives their close;
But the rose's scent is bitterness,
To him that loved the rose.

—FRANCIS THOMPSON

The first time I saw Kamala was at a party given by my father at Anand Bhawan. I was quite a little girl and not allowed to attend the party, but I could watch it from the verandah, which I did. It was an aunt of mine, I think, who pointed out Kamala to me and said, "Do you see that girl and do you think you will like her? She is going to be your sister-in-law." I looked in the direction my aunt pointed out and saw a tall, slim, exceedingly pretty girl sitting with some others at a table. I could not quite understand what a sister-in-law meant, but I guessed she was coming to live with us. I thought it would be nice to have another sister, though I wished she had been younger and nearer my age! I have never forgotten that first picture of her and the utter youthfulness and freshness that were Kamala's when she was seventeen.

Some months later Jawahar's wedding took place in Delhi and Kamala came to live with us. I remember well the pride my parents took in showing off their beautiful daughter-in-law; she was not only pretty, she was the picture of health. Looking at her, one would never have prophesied that she was to spend most of her life on a sick bed. Marriage seemed to start off well for Kamala and Jawahar. The future looked very bright and no clouds darkened the horizon, and a few years of happiness passed. Then suddenly changes started taking place. Politics took hold of Jawahar and also of my father, and many drastic changes took place because a thin half-starved-looking man came into our lives and also into the lives of many others to change the whole course of events. That little man was Gandhiji. Kamala, like the rest of our family, gave up all luxuries and became one of his most devoted followers. He had very great affection for her and she for him and the cause he had made so dear.

Kamala had never known hardship or sorrow. Before she was married and afterwards she had led a life of security and ease with no fear of what the morrow would bring. Suddenly all this changed and it became one of uncertainty, of separation and heartaches and also many physical discomforts. With an unflinching courage Kamala confronted everything smilingly. Not once did I hear a word of complaint or dissatisfaction—no grouse against fate as most of us have when things do not work out the way we want them to. When Jawahar dedicated his life to his country, Kamala did not hesitate a second to fall in beside him. If ever India had a super-soldier with thoughts only for the country and none for self, with an energy that never flagged and a courage the like of which one rarely comes across, that soldier was Kamala. Little is known of Kamala, and as a friend of mine has written about her, "her life was like the luminous flame of an oil lamp. It wavered, it brightened, it grew in intensity all the time and then quietly when the oil got drained the flame flickered and died." It is said that "whom the gods love, die young," and this must be so; for no one could help loving Kamala or admiring her pluck. Living as she did, over-shadowed by strong personalities like her husband's and her father-in-law's, she still made a place for herself in politics, and might have attained much fame if death had not snatched her away so cruelly. She was frail to look at, but her character was strong and true. Few people except those who knew her very well knew the strength that lay behind those gentle eyes or that quiet manner of hers. She had many virtues but many faults too. She was child-like to a fault and never seemed to have grown out of her girlhood days. At times she was terribly neglectful of her health and no amount of good advice given would make her take more care of herself. In spite of many illnesses which almost cost her her life, she never seemed to age. Till the end she retained the sweet girlish looks and figure that she had when she was married. Ill health caused havoc with her body internally but externally she barely changed during all the years I knew her.

For years after Kamala's marriage I saw very little of her. As a new bride, she was always being feted, and later on she was kept occupied with social activities, as my father entertained a great deal and, Mother being more or less an invalid, Kamala acted as hostess for him. In 1926, when we were together in Europe, I really got to know Kamala well and we became great friends. We used to have long and sometimes very heated discussions on various things in life that concerned us or on what we had read or heard about, especially women's rights, but they always ended pleasantly. She was confined to bed most of the time in Europe. The few months of companionship we had together when she was able to travel about were grand. She was always eager to see new things, to learn something new. She enjoyed a picnic or a party to the fullest extent and never acted like a spoil-sport, no matter how weary she felt. She never complained, however grave the provocation. On our return from Europe we came closer together, for we both took an active part in politics and worked together. Here again I marvelled at Kamala's energy. I, who was far more healthy than she, often gave in to fatigue or weariness and stayed at home, but not she. At 5 a.m., on a cold winter's day, she used to be up and ready, as we had to have drill for the women volunteers at that hour, and then from 8 a.m. our daily work of picketing foreign cloth shops started. Throughout the cold months of winter Kamala continued the usual routine and worked all day long. Then summer came and she still kept at her post in spite of the blazing sun and the terrible heat. Many of us did the same but we often grumbled and felt tired and disheartened. Not so Kamala, whose faith and spirits never seemed to flag. But tiring herself out in this manner she hastened her end, for though her spirit was strong, her pain-racked body could not stand the strain and in the end death conquered.

Though a very quiet and unobtrusive person, Kamala had very definite views on life and once her mind was made up, she acted with a determination which ill health would not shake. She was naturally over-shadowed by Jawahar to some extent, but not entirely so, for she had a personality of her own.

Kamala was an ardent feminist and many were the battles she fought for the rights of women among her friends and workers. Often she landed herself in trouble with the menfolk, because they said that their wives had been listening to Kamalaji and imbibing her views which did not suit them at all. She had a spirit that was most independent and that no hardship or sickness could conquer. She was proud of the fact that she had been able to play even a small part in her country's struggle for independence, and was happy in the knowledge that Jawahar was the beloved of millions. She never grudged him his fame and was never jealous of his admirers.

From 1934 onwards Kamala's health deteriorated rapidly. She was sent to a sanatorium in Bhowali. We spent many anxious days hoping and praying for the best, but she gradually got worse. Jawahar was once again back in prison. This time he was in Almora and was allowed to visit Kamala now and then at given intervals. How much she must have looked forward to them and how fleetingly the hours they spent together must have passed! At last the doctors suggested that Kamala should go to Switzerland. Raja and I had gone up to Bhowali to be with her for some time before she left. I had a son hardly two months old and Kamala was even more overjoyed to see him than my mother had been. She threatened me then that on her return she would take my little son away from me and bring him up if I myself did not do so properly.

On the day fixed for her departure, Jawahar was allowed to

come from Almora Jail to see her off. What thoughts kept passing through his mind on that agonizing day I cannot say; but to watch his face was heart-breaking. His eyes held all the sorrow which he tried in vain to hide by a stern expression. As the moment came to bid farewell, he and Kamala did so, each with a brave smile. Then her car took her down the hill to the train which was to take her to Bombay. Jawahar, after embracing Mother and me, with unshed tears in his eyes, got into the waiting car that was to take him back to the Almora prison. As he turned his back on us and walked away, he seemed suddenly to have lost the spring in his walk and the energy he always had. He looked utterly worn out and much older than he had been a few hours ago.

Some months later Jawahar was released and flew to Europe because Kamala's condition was bad, and on February 28, 1936 she died in Badenweiler, a small town in Germany, with Jawahar and Indira by her side.

II.

Some shadows, some sunshine, some triumphs, some tears,
And a gatherin' weight o' the flying years.

—EDEN PHILLPOTTS

Jawahar returned to India after Kamala's death in March 1936, leaving Indira behind at school in England. I was anxious to go and see him but could not do so for some time, until my baby was one month old. It was a painful journey and I dreaded meeting my brother after the tragic death of Kamala

Being very fond of her myself, I keenly realized how great was Jawahar's loss.

As we arrived at Anand Bhawan, Jawahar came out to meet us. His face, which a few months ago had looked so youthful, was aged and lined with sorrow. He looked desperately tired and worn out. Though he tried hard to hide the anguish of his heart, his sad expressive eyes held a world of agony that hurt those who were constantly with him. We stayed a couple of weeks in Allahabad and then went to Lucknow with the rest of the family to attend the Congress which was being held there.

Jawahar had been elected president of the Congress session that year. As usual, politics occupied his time and personal loss and sorrow were put aside. Though sad and lonesome, Jawahar engrossed himself with innumerable conferences and all kinds of other work. He was again elected president for the following year when the Congress met at Faizpur.

After the Faizpur Congress, general elections were being held throughout the country for the Provincial Legislatures. Jawahar threw himself into a whirlwind campaign for the Congress candidates. He toured the country from one end to another, addressing hundreds of meetings in towns and villages, and thereby he succeeded in reviving the enthusiasm of the people, who were just recovering from the last struggle. The Congress gained large majorities in seven provinces and after considerable discussion accepted ministerial offices in the provinces as a result of an agreement with the Viceroy. Almost all the Congress ministers had been for years behind prison bars. My sister Swarup also became a minister—the first and only woman minister in India.

From her childhood Swarup had been a very tactful person and was eminently suited to become a minister. She seldom if ever gets agitated over anything and deals with all kinds of situations in a calm unruffled manner. Charming, self-possessed and beautiful, she has little difficulty in winning people over. As a minister she was a great success. It was a difficult task she undertook to perform, never having been trained for any work of that type, but she excelled at it and was very popular. When Swarup started taking an active part in politics her ability as a speaker surprised us all. She seemed to have been born to it and seldom showed any signs of nervousness no matter how large the gathering which she had to address. She speaks with fluency and ease both in Hindustani and English.

When still quite young Swarup's hair had started to become grey—a family weakness—and all too rapidly it became more and yet more white. Now she has almost silvery white hair but it only enhances her loveliness. She is a capable mother and an efficient housewife. In spite of the fact that politics take up a great deal of her time, she still finds time to look after her home and children.

Jawahar used to come to Bombay two or three times a year and stay with us. We loved having him but saw very little of him as he was usually busy with countless engagements. The quiet routine of our little home changed completely when he was with us. From early morning till long past midnight a stream of visitors used to come and go, some by appointment and others just for a glimpse of Jawahar. The telephone rang incessantly, as did also the doorbell, and I spent most of my time between the two. There were no regular meal hours, no privacy. I never knew how many people would drop in for lunch or dinner, and had to have a fairly flexible kitchen which would cater at a moment's notice for ten to twenty people.

Life was just one long breathless rush all the time. Jawahar was visible only at meal times unless we accompanied him to one of his meetings. On the rare occasions when we had him all to ourselves we spent some delightful hours listening to interesting anecdotes that Jawahar related, talking, laughing and discussing things in general and sometimes our family matters in particular. Often when he spent a quiet evening at home Jawahar would recite or read some poems to us. It is a delight to listen to him, for he does it beautifully.

In January 1938 my mother died suddenly of a paralytic

stroke, and twenty-four hours after her death our aunt, her elder sister, also died of the same kind of stroke. This double tragedy was a terrible blow to all of us. Fortunately I was in Allahabad when it happened. I returned to Bombay rather stunned and miserable. I knew home would never be the same again without Mother, for something of the old life seemed to have gone, never to return.

Later in the year Jawahar was going to Europe to see Indira. Raja and I wanted to go too, but at the last moment he was unable to leave his work. He suggested my going with Jawahar but I did not like the idea of going without Raja and also leaving my two small sons behind. Besides, I had always planned to visit Europe with Raja. I was sorry I did not go with my brother, for he went to Spain while the civil war was on and had an exciting and interesting trip. On his return he brought Indira back with him for a brief vacation.

In April 1939 Indira decided to return to England to continue her studies. Once again Raja and I made plans to go on a trip round the world and to accompany Indira on part of the journey, but our plans fell through, because Raja did not wish to leave his work in the National Planning Committee just then. We cancelled our passages at the last moment and hoped we would be able to go at a later date in spite of the war clouds that threatened the horizon. But we never got the chance, for war broke out and then it was not possible to go.

Towards the end of 1940 Indira decided to come back home for good. She had been in Switzerland for sometime after a severe illness. When I heard she was returning by the first available plane, I was glad but also a little anxious, and I conveyed my anxiety to Jawahar, who was in Dehra Dun Jail. With characteristic promptness he took me to task for behaving like an old woman and being nervous. He wrote back, "I am glad Indu has decided to return. There are all manner of risks and dangers of course but it is better to face them than to feel isolated and miserable. If she wants to return, she must do so and take the consequences."

12.

We watched her breathing thro' the night
Her breathing soft and low,
As in her breast the wave of life
Kept heaving to and fro.
Our very hopes belied our fears,
Our fears our hopes belied.
We thought her dying when she slept
And sleeping when she died.
For when the morn came dim and sad,
And chill with early showers,
Her quiet eyelids closed, she had
Another morn than ours.

—THOMAS HOOD

My mother was a very lovely woman. She was a tiny, dainty little person hardly five feet tall, a typical Kashmiri type, perfect in form and feature like an exquisite doll; but there was nothing doll-like about her, as later years proved.

She was the youngest in her family and had two elder sisters and one brother. Her eldest sister, who was ten years her senior, had brought her up and they were devoted to each other.

Being the youngest and the most beautiful of the three sisters, mother was petted and pampered by her family and treated more like a fragile doll than like a normal girl of her age. She was married when she was quite young and went to her husband's home, a home full of strangers, some kind, others harsh. My grandmother was a great old lady in many ways, but lived up to the tradition of all mothers-in-law. Life was not very happy for Mother till the joint family broke up and Mother reigned mistress of her home. But even in her own home she was treated as though she were a priceless gem, and Father spared no money to surround her with every luxury and comfort that a woman's heart could wish for. Yet with everything in the world one could desire, she lacked the most important thing to a human being—health.

Ever since Jawahar was born Mother kept indifferent health, falling seriously ill every now and then. Naturally, with each illness she became weaker and weaker, and no treatment seemed to cure her. Father took her to Europe to be treated by the best physicians there, but it was all of no avail. I hardly remember a time when Mother was hale and hearty, able to eat, drink and lead a normal life like the rest of us. I did not know what it was to have a Mother's constant care, for she had to be taken care of herself all the time.

And so the years passed. To me Mother seemed to be an exquisite and rare flower to be loved, cherished and protected from all harm and from the petty worries of life. Till 1920, surrounded by every luxury, love and care, Mother reigned queen over her little domain, proud of her illustrious husband, her brilliant son and her home. Sorrow had hardly touched her, nor did worries assail her till the advent of non-co-operation. And then, in a few short weeks, the habits of a life-time were put aside and a minor revolution took place in our small household.

For the rest of us it was not so difficult to adjust ourselves to new conditions. But for Mother and Father it meant changing their whole outlook on life as well as their habits. It was not a very easy task when one was nearing sixty. Yet the suddenness with which my parents gave up the old life and took to the new one left everyone astounded. Father had loved the good things of life—smart clothes, good food and a luxurious way of living. Mother had never worn anything but the finest saris. Never had she had to do without things she wanted, nor did she know what hardships meant. Yet without any hesitation, she had taken to khadi and wore coarse ugly saris whose weight she could hardly bear.

Heartache, sacrifice and endless worries were Mother's lot for the rest of her life, parted by grim prison walls from those she loved best. But the little mother we considered too delicate to do anything proved to us that her frail body held a courage and determination that no amount of hardship or sorrow could break.

The years that followed were very difficult for her. Yet we never heard one word of complaint or regret at the change that had taken place so late in her life, breaking its ordered routine of security and peace into uncertainty and hardships. Strangely enough, in spite of all this Mother managed to keep fairly well. After Father's death she was completely broken. Being very orthodox at heart, she believed that she must have committed some terrible sin in a previous birth to have her husband taken away from her in this life. Besides, she had always been the weak and ailing one and had always imagined that she would die first, as was the right and proper thing for a Hindu wife to do. Father had never known a day's illness. It was jail life with all its privation that had brought him to a premature end.

Almost fifty years they had lived together and shared their joys and sorrows. Mother always depended on Father's strength to help her through every mental and physical crisis. He protected her with his love and care throughout the happy as well as the difficult days they had to face together. Without him Mother was dazed and lost. For a long time she could not adjust herself to circumstances. Jawahar was the perfect son during these days. With his own feeling of loss overpowering him almost to breaking point, he did everything in his power to lessen the blow for Mother. His gentleness and devotion to her during those days were something one cannot describe, for it is too sacred to talk about.

Mother continued to exist, but only for her children, especially Jawahar. Kamala's death dealt another blow to her and left her no strength to face life's problems. Day by day she grew weaker and still weaker.

In 1938 I went with my children on my annual visit to Allahabad and stayed a month. When I was due to return to Bombay, Mother insisted on my putting off the day again and again. One evening we were all together—Jawahar, Swarup, her husband, their children and I. Mother had been feeling stronger and brighter the last few days and especially that evening she seemed quite vivacious.

She sat with us while we had our dinner and was in a reminiscent mood. She talked more than usual and we were happy to see her thus. After dinner we sat and chatted till about 10:30 p.m. Swarup was due to go to Lucknow that night at midnight and Mother informed us that, as she did not feel sleepy, she would sit up till it was time for Swarup to leave for the station. We tried to dissuade her but she would not listen. So we sat and talked. Mother gradually became quieter and quieter.

At 11 o'clock Swarup got ready to go and went to her to say goodby. As Mother rose to embrace Swarup she suddenly crumpled and would have fallen down had Jawahar and I not gone to Swarup's assistance immediately. We helped her to her bed, but even before we laid her down she became unconscious. Mother had had two attacks of paralysis before and this was apparently the third. The doctor was sent for but he shook his head and said there was no hope. She would die in a few hours.

I never knew death could come this way and I was stunned. How could my little mother go away so suddenly and forever without a word or kiss of farewell? She who would never let any of us go out of the house for even an hour without kissing us goodby? It just did not seem possible. I would not accept the doctor's verdict and I was angry because he did nothing— just waited like the rest of us.

All throughout the night we watched beside our mother's bed—Jawahar, Swarup and I and also my aunt Bibi Amma. At five in the morning suddenly Mother's difficult breathing stopped and she lay quiet and at peace as though asleep. Gently in a whisper with tears in his eyes Jawahar said, "She's gone, too"; and then it struck me with all the anguish I vainly tried to curb that the lovely, adored little Mother had gone to sleep from which there was no awakening. Tearless I stood with the others around her bed not daring to breathe. My aunt was not in the room when Mother died, so Jawahar and Swarup went to break the news to her. I stood alone near Mother and suddenly the tears came in torrents which I could not control. Slowly I went down on my knees beside her and bade a silent farewell. Then I rushed out of the room, afraid that my sobs might disturb her.

Thousands upon thousands came to Mother's funeral. We decked her out with flowers, and how beautiful she looked! The lines and wrinkles on her face disappeared leaving it smooth and lifelike. One could hardly believe she was no longer alive.

Gloom and sorrow pervaded Anand Bhawan once again. Bereft of its mistress, it looked sad and desolate.

13.

Some had name and fame and honour,
Learned they were and wise and strong;
Some were nameless, poor, unlettered,
Weak in all but grief and wrong.

—WILLIAM MORRIS

My eldest aunt, whom we called Bibi Amma, was a child widow and, not having any other interest in life, had devoted herself to my mother. They were very different from each other, these two sisters. The elder, having suffered early in her youth, had grown up into a quiet, efficient young woman who realized that life would not be easy for her and that she must learn to look after herself and depend on no one. With this end in view she tried to equip herself mentally to live in a world that was harsh and cruel, and not to be at its mercy. She succeeded, for she was exceptionally clever and very intelligent. She knew not a word of English but had studied Sanskrit and was quite a scholar. She was also quick to grasp business of any sort. Father always used to say that had Bibi Amma been given the necessary education and opportunities she would have made a fine lawyer. She was immensely shrewd and alert and had a magnificent sense of humor.

Being a widow, she had no home of her own and stayed with various relations. A great part of each year she spent with us and we loved having her. While she was with us, she usually helped Mother with her house-keeping, or if Mother was ill she nursed her day and night with no thought of herself. Her world was composed of her sister, her nephews and nieces. Her brother, of whom she had been very fond, had died many years ago. But the main pivot round which her life revolved was my mother. I have never known such unstinting devotion as Bibi Amma had for Mother.

I was her favorite niece. When I was a little girl I loved to sit beside her and listen to all kinds of stories and sometimes fairly tales or tales of the glories of ancient India and of her gallant sons and daughters. Somehow I always imagined that Bibi Amma could have played the part of any of the heroines I read or heard about whose names are immortal. She seemed to have a fearlessness and kind of courage which are rare and which few women possess. I loved her very dearly.

Though ten years older than my mother and having lived an orthodox life, Bibi Amma was far more broadminded. She used to get rather shocked by modern ways and ideas—as Mother did—but she wisely refrained from passing judgment on any of us. Bobbed hair and sleeveless blouses were very sore points with her, but when we teased her about it and tried to get her to disapprove of any of us, she just ignored us. Mother, on the contrary, voiced her objection and showed her disapproval in many ways which did not help matters much. She never insisted on our doing anything we did not like, but she wished we were more orthodox and not quite so modern.

To me especially Bibi Amma was more than a dearly loved aunt. She was my confidant, and sometimes when I hesitated to go to Mother, I went to her fearlessly, knowing that she would try to understand my point of view, however difficult it might be for her to do so.

Mother had always depended on others for guidance and had never had occasion to make up her mind about anything. So she always found it difficult to give us any definite advice. Besides, all of us looked upon Mother as someone frail and lovely whom we had to protect and care for, not someone who was to care for us and guide us. So with all my little troubles and worries I used to go to Bibi Amma and never once did she fail me.

When Mother died and we broke the news to her she was too stunned to believe us. How could it be possible that she should be alive and well and her younger sister die in just a few hours? Gradually her mind grasped the tragic fact. Her strong courageous heart that had withstood so many sorrows suffered a tremendous shock which no human power could alleviate. Yet though her heart bled and her senses reeled, even in her anguish she thought of us first and tried to hide her own grief so as to lessen ours. Realizing that we did not know what arrangements to make for the funeral, she took it upon herself to make all the necessary preparations. With her own hands she got everything ready for the last rites to be performed for the little sister whom she had brought up and cared for all the days of her life.

The funeral cortège left the house, and Bibi Amma stood on the verandah like a statue, neither moving nor shedding a single tear, gazing till she could gaze no more at the flower-decked bier that was taking away the loved sister. Quickly she turned away and walked back to Mother's room. I followed her and found her standing looking as though for the last time at all the things that had been dear to her sister. I put my arms around her and said, "Bibi Amma, will you not lie down and rest a little?" She looked at me still tearlessly and, ignoring my question, she merely said, "Go and have a bath and come down. I shall have some tea ready for you." It was past 2 o'clock in the afternoon. I did not wish to argue. So I went up to my room, bathed and came down to find tea ready. I could not drink it. Bibi Amma's stunned appearance had worried me; so I went in search of her. I found her lying in Mother's room just where Mother used to be. I bent down and called out to her and she opened her eyes. "Bibi Amma," I said, "please have a little tea. It will help." There was no reply. "Bibi Amma, you have always been a mother to us all," I said, "and now you are our mother. We have only you, and I need you desperately." Her arms went round me and with tears filling her eyes for the first time she said "Beti [daughter], to me you have always been a dearly loved daughter, but one can have only one mother and yours has gone forever. I can never take her place.

Besides, I lived for her and now what is there to live for? My task is done. I, too, must go." I could not speak, for the tears I tried vainly to hold back choked me. I sat by her side stroking her head for some time. Then as she seemed to have fallen off to sleep I quietly left her. Several times I went to see her, but each time I found her asleep. At last I grew a bit alarmed. So I went and shook her but she did not wake up. Again and yet again I called to her but she did not move. My brother had not returned from the funeral, so I went and told my sister. She, too, was alarmed and we sent for the doctor.

Jawahar returned at about 7 o'clock and the doctor came too. He saw Bibi Amma and said she had had a stroke, the same as Mother. We could hardly believe it, for never had she had a stroke before nor had she ever in her life been seriously ill. She had always been so strong, and yet she lay unconscious and there was nothing one could do to save her. Everyone was very upset but I most of all, because to me she was infinitely more dear and precious than she had been to others. All we could do was to wait and watch and pass another night as we had passed the previous one. Too miserable to move, I sat beside her, memories flooding my mind of all the days and years she had been with us. Of all the love and understanding she had given me and of her unwavering devotion to Mother and our family, I felt as though my very heart would crack up into a thousand agonized bits but no such relief came and I sat and gazed at her calm face and wondered why such things should happen.

All through the night we watched and at 5 the next morning, exactly twenty-four hours after Mother's death, Bibi Amma passed away. It seemed impossible that our mother and our aunt should both die within twenty-four hours of each other, leaving us utterly lost and desolate.

And so another funeral took place, so different from the one that had taken place a day before. Bibi Amma had taken 'Sanyasa.' No funeral rites were performed. We dressed her in a saffron sari with no other ornament but her own beauty.

Lined and aged though her face was, it suddenly seemed to have become youthful and the wrinkles disappeared. Her face showed such peace that one could not help feeling that she was happy and at rest, perhaps with the sister from whom even death could not part her.

At Mother's funeral thousands had gathered. Like a queen she was carried to the cremation ground with much pomp and splendor. At Bibi Amma's funeral too, a great many people assembled. But what struck one most was the ever increasing crowd of poor people, ragged, old and infirm who came in vast numbers to pay their last respects to her whom they considered a "Devi." One and all they had loved her. No matter how poor or how lowly a man or woman was, unhesitatingly he or she would go to Bibi Amma for advice or help and it was never lacking. She had lived a simple life and shared everything with those she loved, giving freely to the poor and needy. By her death they felt they had lost a great friend. Dying as she did a day after Mother, when to all appearances she was hale and hearty, made people look upon her as a saint, for who else could have given up her life in such a manner?

I marvelled to see our compound full of poor people falling over each other in order to catch a glimpse of the face of her whom they had loved. Not an eye was dry, not a heart that did not grieve that day, as the simple undecorated bier was taken away in a silent procession.

And so I silently bade farewell to the beloved aunt. I knew it was the best thing that could have happened to her, for life without her sister would have been unbearable for her. Yet I wished she had not left us so suddenly, creating a double void which not even the passing of the years could ever fill.

14.

In July 1939 when Jawahar decided to go to Ceylon and asked me to accompany him, I eagerly accepted. I had always wanted to visit Ceylon, but had never got the chance to do so before.

Jawahar was going on a mission. There had been a lot of misunderstanding between Indians and Singhalese which had caused much bitterness. It was therefore decided that Jawahar should go and see things for himself and if possible bring about some sort of harmony between the two peoples.

On a dull misty morning Jawahar and I took off in a small plane from the Poona airdrome. Though it was very early in the morning, a crowd had assembled to see us off—Congress officials, admirers and friends of Jawahar. We went via Hyderabad (Deccan) where we had a delightful lunch with Mrs. Sarojini Naidu and her family, then via Madras and Trichinopoly, reaching Colombo the next day. As we flew over Mount Lavinia airdrome we saw large crowds of people assembled below. Our pilot, a clever and charming young man, did not land immediately. He turned the plane round and flew lower and lower, circling above the crowd. Then he made the plane rise and swooped down again as if in salutation. As soon as we landed, there was a rush towards the plane and the crowd was controlled with great difficulty. People came forward to greet Jawahar and the hearty handshakes and warm smiles of greeting made us feel at home and among friends.

The display of affection shown us by both Singhalese and Indians, standing shoulder to shoulder, seemed to augur well for the mission on which Jawahar had come. Though at the time we thought that Jawahar had succeeded in his work and had eliminated some of the bitterness that seemed to be spreading, the future showed all too plainly that it could not be so. A month after our visit the Ceylon Government dismissed eight hundred Indian employees and sent them back to India.

I loved Ceylon and everything I saw there. In spite of a very busy program, Jawahar always found time to do a bit of sight-seeing. We saw some lovely temples and gardens and were overwhelmed with hospitality wherever we went. Singhalese and Indians vied with one another in almost killing us by kindness. And I wondered how it was possible for such kind and good-natured people to have differences which were creating so much trouble.

Though there is no "purdah system" or segregation of women in Ceylon, at most functions soon after we arrived and had been garlanded our host took charge of Jawahar and escorted him to the men's group while our hostess took me to the women's. Only at meals we mixed for a short while and then somehow the men and women separated again.

In India we have had no suffragette movement. There are certain women's organizations which have mostly concerned themselves with social reforms. But the great impetus to be free and equal with their menfolk came from the national movement. The technique of the non-violent struggle was such that women could play their part shoulder to shoulder with their men. Gandhiji's doctrine appealed to them and showed them a way of breaking age old customs as well as serving their motherland. Thousands of women came out of the seclusion of their homes to face hardships and danger, imprisonment or death, and have found both political and social emancipation.

Wherever we went in Ceylon thousands upon thousands of people assembled to see and hear Jawahar. They were mostly Tamil laborers, men and women, who worked on tea estates and rubber plantations. All along the route they stood patiently for hours to catch a glimpse of Jawahar. As I sat and watched them from the car, or sometimes when I got down and stood with my brother, I looked at the faces around me, faces aglow with love and trust for him who had come from the old motherland, bringing a message of hope and cheer. Jawahar's presence among them seemed to assure them that though they were far away from the land of their birth they were not forgotten.

When I saw Jawahar utterly fagged out at the end of a busy day, I often wondered whether all this was worth while, but I wondered no longer when I saw those faces around me. Every hardship was worth while if it brought such love and confidence of millions with it.

After innumerable meetings, receptions, sightseeing and ten days of ceaseless activity our visit came to an end, or rather Jawahar's did, for I stayed on for another week and then returned to Bombay.

Soon after his return Jawahar decided to go to China. Raja, the children and I went to Allahabad to bid him God-speed. It had always been Jawahar's dream to go to China, for ancient lands have a great fascination for him. I for one was glad that at last he could satisfy this desire. His visit was brief and had to be cut short rather abruptly owing to the outbreak of war. He returned home full of great admiration for the courage and determination of the Chinese people and their great leader, Generalissimo Chiang Kai-shek, to defend the freedom of their country at all costs.

In September 1939 war was declared between England and Germany. India was also declared at war with Germany, though without the consent of her people. At first we watched the situation with anxiety, hoping that at last imperialism would end—that out of the welter of chaos a new and free India would arise. Gandhiji's and the Congress' sympathies were entirely with the British, and the offer of help and friendship was very genuine. We wanted a declaration of war aims but none was forthcoming. Gradually a sense of frustration and disillusionment took root in the heart of the millions, who had hoped that Britain would, at that critical period in her history, show a change of heart.

In 1940 Gandhiji had no alternative but to start Individual Satyagraha. It was but a moral protest on the part of the entire country. The first volunteer chosen by Gandhiji was Vinoba Bhave, the perfect Satyagrahi. The second volunteer was to be Jawahar. But long before Jawahar could offer Satyagraha, he was spirited away on his return journey from Wardha to Allahabad somewhere en route and taken to Gorakhpur to stand his trial. He was sentenced to four years' rigorous imprisonment, a sentence that stunned the whole of India but also made her more determined to fight to the bitter end.

Raja was among the first to volunteer, but when he asked Gandhiji's permission, Gandhiji asked him if I liked the idea. If for some reason I did not do so, he said, he would rather Raja did not go to jail. However, with all the growing chaos and disruption around us, I knew Raja would not be happy unless he was able to do his bit, so I agreed.

A month after Raja's arrest I wrote to Bapu asking his permission to offer Satyagraha myself, as it was irksome to be out of the fight. But he refused to allow me, for my children were young and needed looking after. I had no alternative but to abide by his decision.

Raja and I had never been parted before this for more than a fortnight or three weeks, and I missed him sorely. We were allowed an interview once a fortnight and could write each other at given periods. Nevertheless, though I had many good friends around me, I often felt a little lonely. My sons, too, missed Raja a great deal but young as they were, they understood and were proud of him. Sometimes after we had had an interview they got rather worked up and a few tears rolled down their cheeks though they tried hard to keep them back. This time there are no interviews granted and it has created bitterness and resentment even in the hearts of little children.

15.

Not all the armies of all the empires of earth can crush the spirit of one true man. And that one man will prevail.

—TERENCE MACSWINEY

Jawahar was the only child for almost eleven years and was spoiled by our parents to a great extent, especially by Mother. He did not go to school but was taught at home by tutors and, having no brother or sister, for many years he was a lonely child. Fortunately, though Father did spoil him he was also a strict disciplinarian. This prevented Jawahar from becoming too self-conscious.

Even as a little boy, Jawahar had great admiration for Father. To him Father seemed to be the embodiment of all that was fine, courageous and strong, and his one ambition was to grow up like Father! Though he admired Father and loved him deeply, he also feared him a great deal. Jawahar stood in great awe of Father's temper, for once he had been a victim of it and the memory could not easily be effaced. But all of us knew that Father would never punish us unjustly. However, as the years went by, Father controlled his temper more and more, and though it was always there, he had it under perfect control.

So Jawahar grew up, a shy, sensitive child, mixing a great deal with his elders since he had few companions of his own age. At the age of fourteen he went to Harrow, returning to India after finishing his studies at Cambridge in 1912. That is when I first set eyes on him.

For many years my brother remained a stranger to me, one whom I loved, admired and disliked by turns. After some years when the Satyagraha movement started and Jawahar flung himself into politics, I saw more of him and the better I knew him the greater was my admiration for this brother of mine who, I once wrongly thought, was conceited.

As an elder brother Jawahar is perfect. Though he is so much older than my sister and I, he has never laid down the law to us, as a great many elder brothers do. If he has disapproved of anything we have done, he has always talked the matter over with gentleness and tact, making us see for ourselves that we were in the wrong. If we have disagreed, however hurt he may feel, he tries not to show it and never imposes his own views on us. He is not only an adored "big brother" to Swarup and me, but a grand friend and companion who by his affection and understanding has made himself very precious to us. We know he is always there, just as Father was, a pillar of strength on whom we can lean and get support when wearied out by life's little problems and worries. He never offers advice, but is ever willing to help when help and guidance are necessary. He is also a confidant in whom one can confide without fear of being ridiculed or rebuked. Being so utterly human himself, he never fails to understand another's weakness.

After Father's death Jawahar was most concerned about Mother and me. Swarup was married and had a home of her own. Now that Jawahar was head of our little family, he did not wish either Mother or me to feel that we were dependent on him, as is the usual custom in an Indian family. It never occurred to us but it did to him. Father did not leave a will nor did we expect him to, for it would have been most unlike him to have done so. Yet certain things worried Jawahar. He thought that I might not feel as free as I had in Father's lifetime and that I might not like asking him for money, etc. So he wrote me a letter saying that he wished Mother and me to consider ourselves the real owners of Anand Bhawan and all that Father had left. He was only a trustee to look after our affairs and us and we should look upon him as such. He needed very little for himself and his family, so we should not hesitate to carry on as before and to think of him as being there only to help and guide when necessary! No other brother, I feel, would have behaved thus. It is so typical of Jawahar, who lives up to his ideals and never falters.

Like Father, Jawahar has a temper. When I was about fourteen, Jawahar offered to coach me in mathematics, my bête noire. I wasn't at all thrilled at the prospect but there was no getting out of it. I was still a little scared of Jawahar in those days and did not look forward to his losing his temper with me. However, the first few lessons were a great success and I was fascinated by the way Jawahar taught. The subject I had hated with all my heart became one of the most absorbing interest to me and I actually looked forward to my one hour with Jawahar each day. Just as I began to feel more confident and less afraid of Jawahar, things went wrong. One day I must have been very dull for I just could not concentrate or remember anything. This rather irritated Jawahar (and I do not blame him) and he started getting angry. This only helped to drive everything clean out of my mind and I became completely dumb. He shouted a few sentences to me and terrified me out of my wits. Stunned and mortified, I meekly turned to go away. After all, it was not such a crime, I thought, to have forgotten a lesson. I felt unhappy and hurt, and tears which I tried desperately hard to hide welled up as I slowly collected my books. He noticed my tears and in a second his anger disappeared and he was all repentant. Putting his arms around me he apologized, but nothing he could do or say later would induce me to continue my lessons after this episode.

Those who do not know Jawahar very well imagine that he has no other interest in life except politics, reading and writing. These certainly do take up most of his time but he has a great many hobbies and interests to which he cannot devote as much time as he would like to. Any spare time he has from his political work is usually spent in reading, some times in writing too, though the latter he usually does when he is in jail. He loves riding and is a fine rider. Swimming too he is very fond of but seldom if ever gets the chance to avail himself of it. He never goes to a cinema or a theatre unless we force him to, and if it is something really good he quite enjoys himself. But to see him at his best, one should see him with children of all ages. He is very fond of them and they adore him, for no matter how busy he is or how weary, if a child goes to him and persists in asking the why or wherefore of everything, he will never brush him aside but will stop all his work to satisfy the child's curiosity.

It is really a delight to see him after a hard day's work relaxing with his little nephews or nieces or other children. All his cares and worries seem to leave him and he becomes a little child himself, romping about, playing and enjoying himself every bit as much as the children themselves. Most of us cannot do this as we are too self-conscious and do not forget that we are grown-ups. Jawahar can do so because he is simple and human, and that is why children find in him a playmate after their own heart.

Jawahar has one unfailing quality, no matter where he is, in prison or outside, however busy, tired and weary he may be. He seldom forgets a birthday, anniversary or any other important occasion. It is these little acts of thoughtfulness of his that endear him so deeply to those who know him. It happened once that my birthday according to the Indian calendar fell on Oct. 19, 1930. Jawahar remembered it just after his arrest that same day and some days later he wrote to me:

"It has recently occurred to me that the British Government by issuing an order under Sec. 144 on me and by subsequently arresting me on the 19th October forgot a most important event on that day—and the beautiful and artistic gift that I should have made to my dearly beloved sister, did not materialise—this lapse on my part was most unfortunate. But I hasten to correct it. Wherefore, take yourself to a book-shop and choose some volumes containing the wisdom of the ancients, and the faith of the middle ages and the scepticism of the present and the glimpses of the glory that is to be—and take them and pay for them and consider them the belated, but loving gift of a somewhat absent-minded brother who thinks often of his little sister. And read these chosen volumes and out of them construct a magic city, full of dreams, castles and flowering gardens and running brooks, where beauty and happiness dwell and the ills that this sorry world of ours suffers from can gain no admittance—and life will then become one long and happy endeavor, a ceaseless adventure to build this city of magic and drive away all the ugliness and misery around us."

When Jawahar returned from England he was a very polished and charming young man, but rather proud and somewhat spoiled as a rich man's son is apt to be. The years that followed were full of experience for him, and disappointments as well as much sorrow. But all this helped to mellow him and today he is more lovable than ever before. His western education has naturally influenced him considerably and people think him to be more of a European than an Indian in his outlook. But the moral and political chaos of the world through these years of war and starvation has drawn many of us, Jawahar more so, to the deep and vast sources that have inspired the ideas of the people of India and China. His personality today strikes deeper roots into the ancient soil and draws increasing sustenance from the rich past. The peace of mind and lack of bitterness that he has in spite of many a disillusionment are truly Indian. In him the East and the West have blended, the former to show him the way of life and the latter to give him a wider understanding of the impulses that move the destinies of man. His ardent Nationalism has therefore grown into a firm conviction that the true freedom of our people cannot co-exist with tyranny and oppression of other nations. His sensitive mind is as much affected by any happening in any part of Asia or Europe as in India. He is a true soldier of Freedom, and whenever and wherever Freedom is in peril, he is always ready to defend it with all his might.

There are some who think Jawahar is arrogant and over-bearing. They resent it. At times he is so, but by nature he is anything but arrogant or domineering. He would rather be out of the limelight. I am sure he would have more peace of mind if it were possible, but it cannot be. He is somewhat of a dreamer and often when tired out by work he relaxes and gazes into the distance, his eyes look dreamy and he seems to belong to another world. At times his eyes become unutterably sad, and his face, so youthful in spite of his fifty-three years, suddenly ages and looks years older. Life has not been easy for Jawahar and suffering and sacrifice have left their mark on him as on so many others who have taken the same path.

There are people who find fault with Jawahar and criticize him, but they just do not understand him nor can they fathom his ways. He is human like the rest of us and has weaknesses that most human beings have. Only where the majority succumbs he does not; hence his greatness. If India idolizes Jawahar to-day it is not for his virtues and strength and courage alone but for his very human qualities. He considers himself neither a hero nor a martyr, but just one who has been privileged to serve his country in her hour of need and who will continue to do so till the very end. He does not consider going to jail a great sacrifice on one's part or something to make a fuss about, though almost half his life has been spent in jail. It is inevitable when we are fighting for our freedom against alien domination. He once wrote to me from jail, "Going to jail is a trivial matter in the world today, which is being shaken to its foundation. As a mere routine, I think it has some value and does one good but that value is not very great unless there is an inner urge to do it. If an inner urge is present, little else matters for that represents something vital."

And yet going to jail again and yet again is no easy matter. Nor is jail exactly a bed of roses where one would like to relax every now and then. Some people think that those who have been in prison many times get used to the idea and do not mind it. A few months in jail would soon clear up this misconception. Physical discomforts there always are and one expects them when one goes to prison. It is the mental adjustment that is difficult when one has to cope with the daily petty tyrannies of jail life.

To be separated from one's dear ones, to meet them only when it pleases the authorities, all goes to make one feel irritable and sometimes bitter. To stay for any length of time in jail and not get embittered is indeed a great achievement and Jawahar has successfully done this.

As Jawahar wrote to me, if there is an inner urge to do a certain thing, then only can one go through any hardship or suffering to attain one's goal. We have often been worried when Jawahar has been rearrested but he has always given us courage and strength to face whatever might befall him by treating his own case lightly.

In 1940 Jawahar was sentenced to four years' rigorous imprisonment. The vindictiveness of the sentence stunned each and every human being who read about it. To us, too, it came as a great blow. Used though we were to strange and unexpected edicts of the Government, this hit us harder than any previous convictions of Jawahar's had done. I was terribly upset and showed it in one of my letters to Jawahar in which I also asked him if Raja and I could come and interview him at Dehra Dun where he had been kept. In reply to my letter Jawahar wrote:

"Raja and you will of course be very welcome whenever you come. I should like to see Raja, especially as I may not have a chance of doing so for some time to come [Raja was going to offer individual Satyagraha sometime later]. I was sorry to learn that he was rather put out on learning of my conviction and you too, my dear. I have seldom felt quite so peaceful in mind as I have done lately, and that is some feat in this mad world of ours. Through some practice I have learned to draw myself in and shut the various drawers of my mind which relate to activities which have been suspended. You must not worry unnecessarily about me. Life becomes harder for all of us and the soft days of the past already belong to an age that is gone. When will they return, or will they ever return? No one knows. We must adapt ourselves to life as it is and not hunger for what is not. Physical risk and suffering are after all petty compared to the troubles and tempests of the mind. And whether life is soft or hard, one can always get something out of it; but to enjoy life ultimately, one must decide not to count the cost."

From childhood Father had taught us not to be afraid of taking risks or facing dangers. "Safety first" has never been our motto nor I hope will it be that of our children. Many a time each one of us has had to undertake a task or a journey where risk and danger was involved, but this never prevented us from going through with our program. As far as Jawahar is concerned, if there is even a suspicion of danger attached to any work, it is an added inducement for him to take it in hand. Perhaps at times it might seem a little childish, but it is better to have this attitude towards things than to live in fear all one's life because each step one takes might be risky.

Once Jawahar was in prison in Alipore, Calcutta. We had not heard from him since he was arrested, so were naturally a little anxious. At that time I received another letter from him, a very typical one. "My dear, I hope you and the others are not worried about me. I am well and *J'y suis, j'y reste*. I shall read a lot, for indeed there is little else to do—just to read and to think and go through the day's routine. So when I come out —and that is a long way off—I may be a little wiser than I am, perhaps and perhaps not. Wisdom is a very elusive thing and difficult to seize. And yet sometimes it comes suddenly and unawares. Meanwhile I shall be a faithful votary and seek her good will. Some day she may show me favor. Anyway, jail is not an unsuitable place to woo her. The hurly-burly of life seems far off and does not distract and it is good to see the life of everybody from a little distance—detached."

Jawahar has a great love for outdoor life, not that he gets much chance to avail himself of it. He is exceedingly fond of winter sports and spent hours skiing or skating in Switzerland when we were there together. He loves nature in all her fresh and unspoiled beauty, for he is so essentially a child of nature himself.

Jawahar expects everyone to do things well and efficiently, whether at games or at work, and is a hard taskmaster. For almost six months I acted as his secretary in 1931, and though I enjoyed the work I lived in perpetual dread of making a mistake and incurring his wrath. Luckily I managed to escape it and I have never been able to decide whether it was due to my efficiency or just a fluke. To be slack, inefficient and lazy is an unforgivable sin in Jawahar's eyes. Once in Switzerland he offered to teach me skiing. The day he chose for the first lesson was not a good one. It had not snowed for a couple of days and the previous snowfall had hardened into slippery ice. Every time I stood up in skis down I came with an unpleasant bang. I simply could not keep my balance, much to Jawahar's annoyance. He thought I was afraid and got very annoyed. I tried desperately to take a few steps but each time I fell down, not always elegantly—so Jawahar gave me quite a bit of his mind and prophesied that I would never learn in a million years. Hurt and mortified, I asked a Swiss friend of ours to teach me and within three days I was skiing all by myself, in spite of my brother's prediction.

In a sick room Jawahar is an ideal nurse. His gentleness and understanding are infinite under the most trying circumstances, and his patience is unlimited. His greatest quality is that he always adapts himself to circumstances and finds comfort and beauty in little things around him, which is a great achievement. Once he wrote to me from Dehra Dun Jail:

"The hot afternoon sun has melted much of the snow except on the mountain tops. The clouds have rolled away giving glimpses of that amazing and fascinating thing, the deep blue sky, just after rain in North India. Do you have this in Bombay? Perhaps you have but nobody notices it. The evening was unusually beautiful to-day. The clouds were in a playful mood and they caught the rays of the smiling sun and seemed to hurl them about in reckless abandon. Extraordinary colors came and went, fantastic shapes appeared and disappeared and over all was this riot of color. The bare mountain tops blazed red and they reminded me of the mountains of the Khyber region. Patches of snow were lit up occasionally and then faded away, and soon after the moon, almost full, added to the variety."

Though Jawahar is always smiling and apparently happy, he has had more than his share of heartache and sorrow. To have lost his young wife when he needed her love and companionship most was a terrible tragedy for him. Outwardly he tried not to show how deep was his grief. Only for a few fleeting seconds does Jawahar lose grip on himself, only to regain his poise and unruffled appearance.

At a very young age, Jawahar started to drift into politics, little realizing that it would become his life work. Little by little the course of events swept him along with the tide and he was carried away. But had he his whole life to live over again, Jawahar would do the same things that he has done. He might do them a little differently, that is all. Many accuse him of having fads, of dreaming dreams, of talking about big things and not dealing with the job in front of him. These accusations may or may not be true, but one thing is undeniable: Jawahar is a great dreamer. He dreams of great things of the future, dreams that may not be realized by him but by somebody else. But his dreams are never personal. They are all woven round the future of India—an India of whose coming greatness Jawahar has not the shadow of a doubt and in whose service Jawahar would gladly lay down his life.

16.

Ghost-like I paced round the haunts of my childhood,
Earth seemed a desert I was bound to traverse,
Seeking to find the old familiar faces.

How some they have died and some they have left me,
And some are taken from me, all are departed,
All, all are gone, the old familiar faces."

—CHARLES LAMB

I was on my way to Allahabad with my two little sons, Harsha and Ajit. Raja was going to follow us later. We were going to attend Indira's marriage. The journey was a familiar one and I knew almost every landmark by heart. I had travelled by the same route innumerable times during the past nine and a half years but each time I had felt a little uneasy, wondering what news would greet me on my arrival, for something unexpected and unpleasant always happened. Either Mother was suddenly taken ill or Jawahar had been arrested, and so on. But this time I looked forward with joy to my visit, for the occasion for which I was going was one of happiness: a very dearly loved niece was going to be married.

We arrived at the Allahabad station at a fairly late hour of the night and drove off in the car that had come to meet us.

After a fifteen-minute drive we saw Anand Bhawan in the distance and as usual I was filled with great love for my old home. Though the hour was late, Anand Bhawan was gaily lit up and seemed to be humming with activity. People were coming and going in and out of the house and servants were busy rushing to and fro. From every room came the sound of voices and laughter and once again after many long years Anand Bhawan wore a festive appearance.

Slowly the car turned into the stately gates and drove up to the porch. As it stopped, forgetful of my children, I jumped out to go in search of my brother, but I had hardly gone a few steps when he came out of a room and embraced me and the children. It felt good to be back in the old familiar surroundings and to see Jawahar, my sister and others again.* Each time I returned to Anand Bhawan, I experienced a thrill, but it was only for a moment. All too soon realization would dawn that the loved home was no longer the same, that so many dear ones were absent and new drastic changes kept on taking place. Tears would rise to the surface but remain unshed. On this occasion, however, I was not going to allow myself to show any signs of sadness, for it was a happy occasion for all of us.

Though the passing of the years had wrought havoc in the home that once was full of happiness and peace, it was still good to be back, to feel the warmth of a brother's love, a sister's care, and to feel a carefree girl of eighteen once again.

The wedding day dawned bright and beautiful. From early morning people were busy seeing that all was in readiness for the marriage ceremony. Many cousins and friends flocked to the bride's room to tease her and joke with her as young girls do, and to be with her while she was dressed in her bridal clothes of fine handspun and hand-woven khadi, spun by her own father during one of his terms of imprisonment. Slightly flushed and a little excited, though pretending to be quite calm, the bride sat surrounded by people and by the hundreds of

* Jawaharlal was at that time out of prison.—*Ed.*

presents which kept on streaming into her room. Lovely to look at, on this special occasion she looked lovelier than ever, frail and almost ethereal. She laughed and talked to those around her but sometimes her big black eyes would darken and hold a distant sorrowful look. What dark cloud could mar the joy of this happy day? Was it due to a longing for the young mother who was no more, by whose absence a void had been created which even on this day remained unfilled? Or was it the thought of parting from the father, a father whose very life she had been? She was leaving him now to a life that would be lonelier for him than it had ever been before. Maybe it was the breaking from all the old ties and the starting of a new life which brought a passing look of sadness to the young bride's eyes, for who could foretell what the future held in store for her—happiness? sorrow? fulfillment? disillusionment? The dark eyes became darker but for a fleeting moment only, then once again they regained their natural look and were unfathomable.

The auspicious hour drew near and Indira escorted by Jawahar came to the pavillion where the marriage was to be performed. The bridegroom awaited her there. The ceremony was simple and short with no unnecessary paraphernalia. The bride and bridegroom sat side by side and opposite sat the bride's father. Beside him was an empty 'asana' (seat) for the wife who, though no more, was so much in his thoughts that day; she had been so much a part of his existence. Looking at that empty seat so full of tragic significance, I felt a lump in my throat as I thought of her. How happy she would have been had she been present! I could almost visualize her, youthful and smiling, eyes sparkling with merriment and joy and looking just a little older than the bride herself. But I tried to put away all sad thoughts of the might-have-beens, for had they remained unchecked they would have come crowding one upon another and it would have marred the day.

For a few days the usual wedding parties continued and the old home seemed to have brightened up considerably. Then one by one the guests started leaving and after some weeks I also returned to Bombay.

* * * *

A year passed. Once again I was on my way to Allahabad, this time to spend one short week with my sister Swarup, who after nine months' imprisonment was out on parole for a fortnight. Late at night I arrived at the familiar station, looking a little more dilapidated than it had done the last time. A friend and a young niece, Swarup's daughter, met me and we drove home, not in a car because there was no car any longer, but in a rather ancient tonga which seemed to crawl along the bad roads.

At last we turned into the gates of Anand Bhawan. The sight that greeted me was very different from the one that had greeted me a year ago. No bright lights shone out, no servants were visible hurrying hither and thither. The house was dark except for one dim lamp in the porch and another peeping through one of the rooms. Our home seemed gloomy, deserted and silent. I had a queer feeling of fear and depression as though I was treading an unknown ground and did not know what to expect round the corner. With a sinking heart I got out of the tonga and went in search of Swarup. As I entered her room she got up to greet me and embrace me. I put my arms around her, trying not to let her see how moved I was at her changed appearance. A year ago I had seen her looking ten years younger than she really was. Nine months she had been in jail and she was out for a few short weeks now. Once more jail had wrought havoc on a loved one and left its mark all too plainly on the face which had aged considerably in those few months.

I stayed a week and then returned to my home, my children and an existence without my dear ones. Swarup had to return to jail for an indefinite period, leaving her three young daughters outside to fend for themselves as best as they could, in a world where bitterness and frustration had taken the place of hope and happiness.

Sitting in the train which was taking me back to Bombay, I wondered when I would next visit Anand Bhawan and what further changes I would find there. Would it ever be like the old home again, full of laughter and happiness? Or would it remain a lonely desolate abode bereft of all joyousness and mirth? I hope it would not be the latter and I sent up a silent prayer that Anand Bhawan would once again be the 'abode of joy' which it was meant to be when Father named it so.

I returned to my small flat in rather a miserable frame of mind. Our little home is home no longer because Raja is not with us, and life, though it needs must go on, is not happy or contented because Jawahar and hundreds and thousands of others lie behind prison bars. For the last four years a war has been going on which has engulfed the whole of humanity. We who were denied our freedom were thrown into this cauldron without even our formal consent. It is a war, we are told, which is going to bring peace and freedom to all mankind. And yet at every step during these four years, we have been denied our right to freedom—freedom even to mobilize our vast resources in men and materials under our own leaders.

Our people were torn between their sympathy for the United Nations and their hatred of imperialism. We therefore asked for a clear declaration of war aims which would assure freedom to all. But we were not given even a reply. In 1942, after many hesitations a promise of freedom after the war was offered to us—a promise hedged and hemmed by conditions which no nation in the world can fulfill. Besides, we have had too many of such promises in the past, not one of which has ever been kept. What a mockery to ask us to shed our blood, to starve our people and to suffer all privations in defence of Democracy and Freedom that have been denied us!

Today we are in the midst of our own struggle for freedom and the right to control our own destinies. We wish to be rid of imperialism not only where it concerns us, but wherever it exists throughout the world. Our freedom is but a symbol of that force, that desire to rid the rest of the world as well as ourselves of foreign domination and exploitation.

The Individual Civil Disobedience Movement of 1941 represented our demand for a clarification of Britain's war aims. It was an appeal to the moral conscience of the world, but it was in vain. Our appeal had to be more insistent and our sufferings greater. Despite the grave danger at our very frontiers, the Congress had to call upon the people to prepare for greater sacrifices, for the issue was not only peace and freedom for all mankind, but also the defence of our country against the fascist aggressors. So the present struggle had to start, though it was not really launched, the leaders having been arrested before the negotiations with the Government were over. Our struggle today for India's independence is not a mere expression of narrow nationalism, but an urge for a wider and truer conception of human freedom. Always the people of India have opposed fascism and imperialism and have extended their meagrely filled hands with whatever little help they could give to China, Spain and other countries. Where they have been unable to help materially they have reiterated their sympathy and faith in the cause of all down-trodden peoples of the world.

The aim before us today and in fact before the whole world is that a fundamental change should take place, political, social and economic, during the war. Only thus can we mobilize our people to defend themselves against Japanese aggression and put India on the road to progress and prevent the deterioration of our country. The whole world is in chaos and it is for us to bring some semblance of peace and order into it. It may not be within the grasp of us in India, but as long as we keep the vision in view and light the torch, others may achieve what we have been unable to do. There may be many pitfalls and many stumbling blocks on the way to the realization of our common goal, but what does it matter as long as our steps lead us in the right direction and our eyes look steadily and unwaveringly in front?

For thousands of us, all over the world and especially for us in India, there can be no rest or peace now till freedom is won, whatever the cost may be. If suffering and hardship are to be the lot of a lifetime, we must resign ourselves to them and carry on with our work, hoping to create a happier world for our children to live in, even if happiness and contentment is denied us. As Pierre Van Paassen writes in his book *That Day Alone*:

"A day will surely come when man, having grown tired of walking alone, will turn to his brother. On the day when we shall have learned to feel the sorrows and the joys, the suffering and the hope of others, as our very own, that world order of love and justice for which the universe yearns and of which the planets in the stillest night are splendid but imperfect symbol, shall have come nearer."

From the time I was born until 1919 life was smooth, tranquil and happy. The first disturbing feature in my placid life was the massacre of Jallianwalla Bagh and it had set me thinking about certain things which I had never bothered about before. It was the first upheaval and later came many more, each one larger than the last. From 1920 onwards life was hardly normal for any of us, but our family remained intact and that was a great thing. In 1931 Father's death not only left a big gap in our lives but seemed to be the beginning of more misfortunes. In 1936 Kamala died and two years later Mother passed away. Financially too, we were not very well off.

Life was not either happy or smooth for any of us, but I think the younger generation suffered because of it more than we did. Constant partings and other misfortunes both big and small have at times been a sore trial and have almost made me despair. What helps me not to lose courage completely or give up hope is the firm conviction and faith in the justice of our cause. It is not only our cause but the cause of the common man all over the world. This thought alone helps me, as I am sure it does so many others, and makes it possible to bear all the sorrows and partings of life without a murmur and without getting embittered.

The instability of life such as the one my family and I have known and continue to bear, along with so many of our countrymen, for so many years, is rather wearing for one's nerves. I go on hoping and waiting for normal times, for a happy reunion and for peace and prosperity for our country, but the future does not look too bright. Yet in spite of all the misfortunes that have come my way—and perhaps they are a little more than one bargained for—, in spite of the sufferings that have been and the trials that still may come, in spite of the turmoil that has been a constant companion throughout my life, I can still look back on all that has happened with no regrets.

> *Though frustrated and disappointed,*
> *Keep watch, India.*

> *　　　*　　　*

> *Be not ashamed, my brothers, to stand*
> *Before the proud and the powerful*
> *With your white robe of simpleness.*
> *Let your crown be of humility,*
> *Your freedom the freedom of the soul.*
> *Build God's throne daily upon*
> *The ample bareness of your poverty*
> *And know that what is huge is not great*
> *And pride is not everlasting.*

> —TAGORE

The following two chapters represent the theme which developed into With No Regrets. *The book ends here but the theme survives. I give these chapters because they are the sheaf of memories that will always haunt me.*

17.

The ten-year-old little girl stood beside her mother's bed gazing down at the new arrival—a little sister, so tiny yet so perfect! Wise beyond her years, she did not ask foolish questions as to how and where the little one had come from. She had a vague idea about it all and there she stood marvelling at Nature's handicraft, and wondering if some day she too would have a little infant as sweet as this one to play with. Her heart went out to the tiny creature, not in sisterly love alone, but with a tenderness and protectiveness that was much more.

The years passed. It was a festive occasion in a noble household and all round were signs of rejoicing. The old house was gaily decorated and sounds of music and laughter were heard from within. The youngest daughter of the house was getting married that day, and there she sat in one of the rooms—just in her teens—looking lovelier than the dawn itself in her pale pink sari. Little did she realize the importance of that day. Beside her sat her elder sister, also young and very beautiful, dressed in a spotless white sari with no ornaments to adorn her, for she was a child-widow. She too had been in her teens when she was married and within a year she had lost the husband she had hardly known. But today there was no room for sorrow or self pity in her heart. Her little sister whom she had practically brought up was getting married and it was a day of great rejoicing. All her devotion was for this sister. For herself she craved nothing—no fine clothes, no lovely jewels, no luxuries. All that she prayed for every day, especially this day, was that no sorrow or pain should cross the beloved sister's path. And as she sat beside the child bride, her sad brown eyes looking lovingly at her, her heart swelled with pride at the lovely picture before her.

The years passed on. The little sister had grown to be a very beautiful woman, a mother of several children, and mistress of a happy luxurious home. And so, many years went by peacefully and contentedly.

Then changes took place in the great house. The master no longer graced it—the mistress was sad and lonesome, and the house that had once been full of laughter and joy, was silent and sorrowful. All the sunshine and happiness seemed to have departed with him who was its very life.

In a corner of the garden sat two aged women—but age had only enhanced the loveliness of their youth. The elder of the two still looked stronger. She had hardly a grey hair and her sad face had an undescribable loveliness that seemed to belong to another world. The younger was still tiny and dainty and very frail. Her almost snow-white hair cast a halo about her face on which sorrow and suffering had left its mark. From the distance the voices of little grand-children were carried to them on the breeze and now and again a smile would light up the two faces as they heard the little ones.

She stood near the bed-side, turned as if to stone, looking down at the calm, sweet face of her younger sister. Very lovely she looked in death—as she had always been in life. But how could she have gone and left her, the elder of the two, to carry on when life's work had ended? It was not possible. How could she who had always been timid and afraid take this long journey alone into the Unknown? She could not let her go alone—she must follow and be with her, to hold her hand, and give her courage. . . .

They had taken her and there was nothing left for the elder sister, nothing but a heart that was broken and bleeding. Quietly she lay down in a corner, dazed and weary. Her eyes closed and all sorts of pictures passed before her mind's eye—a baby sister lying so helplessly beside her mother—a young bride so lovely and so childlike. A radiant mother with her children—an aged sister, weak and frail and then—then someone so like and yet unlike the beloved sister, lying so pale and still as if she were lifeless. But no, she was not dead—it was all a mistake, for there she was beckoning to her elder sister to help her across a stream. A smile lighted up the sister's face—a smile of surpassing tenderness as she stretched out her hand to grasp that of her sister's and help her into another world.

And so they found her with a look of infinite peace upon her face—peace and happiness, for had she not been united to the little sister after just a few hours' separation and followed her to the ends of the earth and beyond? All her life had been one long selfless act of devotion to this sister. Death was not strong enough to keep them apart.

18.

"Memories are like roses in December," said a poet. They are, when they bring with them the fragrance of beautiful flowers to a lonely soul, but not all memories are beautiful. Some are tinged with sadness, some with regret, and others bring an ache which neither time nor environment can change or lessen. One has memories of pleasant days, days of sunshine and laughter. Memories of sad days when the sun seemed to be overshadowed by dark clouds and the life seemed empty and useless. Yet they all pass, because they must—some leaving few traces behind, others that are unforgettable.

And so memories assail me each time I return to the home of my childhood, happy memories of a marvellous childhood, and sad memories of later years—of days gone by which one cannot re-live again. Memories that sadden the heart till it is near breaking point, for the old home is no longer what it was, and each time I return to it some new change has taken place.

I sat in the old familiar garden, the only unchanged spot in a world that is ever changing. Before me stood the stately house that was my home, and as I gazed at it with unseeing eyes, with my thoughts far away, the book I had intended to read lay on my lap neglected. At my feet and round about lovely butterflies flitted. The fresh smell of the grass was good and the scent of roses was wafted along on the breeze towards me. I lay back with a sigh, for though all around me everything looked so beautiful and so peaceful, in my heart there was a dull ache for something beyond my grasp—something that I had lost and could not find again. And so, with my thoughts wandering unconnectedly, I dozed off, to dream of days that had been but were just a memory now.

I saw a house full of people—a large, rambling, old house full of every luxury that taste and money could provide. Its master, a fine looking man with a tremendous personality, seemed to fill the whole house with his presence, his laughter and the love with which he surrounded his family. He seemed to be a tower of strength that stood between those he loved and all harm. The lady of the house, beautiful beyond all description, a fragile, gracious little creature, flitted about looking after her family with an energy one would hardly believe possible in one so frail. Everywhere there was life and activity—happiness and contentment, and in such an atmosphere three children grew up.

Some years later. The house was the same but all signs of pomp and splendor had gone. Simplicity had taken the place of lavish grandeur of a few years before. But the inmates were the same, and the hearty laughter of the master still rang throughout the house and cheered all those who might be feeling downhearted. For the change had come, not through any misfortune, but because of a changed outlook and political convictions.

A few more years passed. It was another house built next to the old one. A house like a dream which a loving father built for a beloved son but which brought little happiness to its inmates, and much sorrow.

In one of the spacious rooms sat an old man with snow-white hair, his head bent in thought. He was very ill, and had travelled hundreds of miles to arrive home before his son was taken away to prison for certain political views that he had held. The old man too had passed many months in prison cells for the same ideas and he was ready to go again. He had arrived in time, just in time to clasp his son by the hand before he was taken away. Near him sat the little woman who had so bravely shared his life and all its triumphs and sorrows. She looked more fragile than ever, yet strangely enough it was she who gave him the courage to bear each new blow, she who had been so timid and frail, while he had always been so fearless and strong.

In one corner of the room sat the elder daughter of the house. She was married and had children and realized fully how much anguish her parents must be feeling. Her eyes were glued to their faces anxiously and her heart was torn with pain to watch their silent suffering and not to be able to help. In another part of the room, leaning up against the wall with her head turned away from the others, stood the younger daughter. In her heart there was an ache also, in her eyes were unshed tears, and her mind was seething with rebellious thoughts. The others seemed to be resigned to whatever the fates might have in store for them—but not she. Sometimes she felt that all that suffering was necessary for a cause as great as theirs. At other times doubts and misgivings flooded her mind when she saw her parents, burdened with anxiety and loneliness. They could have owned the world and lived a live of comfort, free from all cares and worries—yet they chose the difficult path of duty and devoted their lives to served humanity and their country. Tortured with conflicting thoughts she stood, not daring to look at the parents whose sufferings she could not help to lessen. The house was strangely silent without the beloved son, yet even the old house seemed to stand more erectly, as though immensely proud of the son it had sheltered within its walls! The parents sat regardless of time, each longing for him who was only a few miles away in a cold prison cell, while they sat in their palatial home, hating the comforts surrounding them.

Just for a short while they sat, each engrossed in his or her own thoughts, and these thoughts revolving round the same person. For a while only—then, suppressing a sigh, the father rose, his firm chin set in grim determination. He must be up and about and carry on the work his son had been prevented from doing, and so squaring his broad shoulders he walked away. And the little woman, mother of a great son, she, too, got up with a brave smile and an aching heart, to carry on the day's work just as before.

The years passed. A huge crowd of thousands upon thousands of human beings lined the route for miles. Not an eye was dry, not a heart that did not ache as if it had lost something of its very own. They were there to pay homage to the great dead, for the master was no longer in their midst. Always a fighter, he even fought death for many days and nights, to be able to live a few more years to see the result of his life's work. But death triumphed, as it always does in the end, and he passed away. In a room of that once joyous house sat the widow of him who had gone on his last journey, unable even to shed tears, for the shock of separation was great. Near her with his arms around her sat her son, his eyes full of tears, for he had loved his father deeply. He knew not how to comfort his mother, but it was she who comforted him, her strong young son, with a soft clasp of the hand.

Time marched on. The old house had seen many changes and it had still to see many more. Cars stood along the drive and policemen were dotted all over the compound. All these preparations were for the arrest of the two daughters. They had not sat idle all these years but had worked and followed in their father's footsteps, and upheld the tradition of their family. And for this they, too, had to go to prison as their father and brother before. Courteously the officers produced the warrant, smilingly the girls received it, and turned to go inside to collect a few belongings. Just then the little mother came, as fast as her weak limbs could carry her. "What is all this about?" she asked—"Why so many cars and people?" Gently the elder daughter put her arm round the mother and told her. For a moment she weakened and tears filled her eyes as she clasped her daughters and whispered, "I shall be so lonely without you." But it was only for a moment. She straightened her tiny figure and faced this new ordeal with all the courage of a baffled lioness. "I am proud of you," she said, "very proud." "And I am not too old to follow suit," she added with a twinkle in her eye. She clasped her daughters once again and put out her hands to give them her blessings. But that delicate wisp of a body had undergone too much suffering and anguish, and could bear no more. As she raised her hands she fainted away. The girls were driven away in a car to their destination. . . . And life went on as usual.

A prison cell with dark grim walls, within which sat two sisters—drawn closer together now than ever before, with a common bond. They sat leaning against each other, looking through the iron bars at a beautiful red sky which meant a glorious sunset somewhere, beyond those prison walls. Wrapped in thoughts they sat, one longing for her own home, her husband and the little children she had left behind; the other longing to hear that infectious laughter of her father's that never failed to give courage and hope, and to feel the beloved mother's arm around her—the mother who was left alone in a big dreary house.

There was rattling of chains and clanging of doors. What was it all about, the prisoners wondered. A wardress came towards the sisters—a telegram in her hands. Fearfully they took it, then after a second they smiled at each other. So she had kept her word, their brave little mother, and she too was behind prison bars in some distant prison. How very courageous of her, and how ruthless of them that took her—an old woman of sixty-five!

A few more years had passed. Large crowds had gathered again in the house that had seen so much of joy and sorrow. It was the little mother who had sighed one evening and given up her life, quietly without a word. She had always lived for others—she died without troubling anyone. And there she lay on her bed, lovely and so lifelike, decked with flowers like a queen, for she was one to the very end.

I saw a lonely house stripped of all its laughter and joy standing in the midst of a garden that was no longer cared for. Inside in one of the rooms sat the son, working, ever working at his table. He had not had an easy life, nor would he have much comfort or leisure in the future, for he had chosen for himself the straight and narrow path, and there was no turning back. Now and then when he raised his tired eyes, one could see a look of indescribable sadness therein, for he was a very lonely man. But he hid his great loneliness if others were present and with his smile and never failing charm of manner he won his way into all hearts.

Uneasily I shifted in my sleep, with my heart as heavy as lead. The years had brought many changes to this home I loved so much, but it was good to know that the brother I had come to see was still out of prison, for home was never quite the same without him. I opened my eyes with a longing to run upstairs to his room and talk to him. I picked up my book and almost ran towards the house. As I entered, the telephone rang. I picked it up and a strange voice said, "This is just to inform you that your brother's trial will be held tomorrow." "The trial tomorrow? What trial?" I wondered. I could not adjust my sleepy brain to the news. Then like a flash it all came back. There was no brother upstairs, waiting for me—I had been dreaming, for he had been arrested two days before.

Wearily I went up to my room and instead of having a brother as a companion, I had only memories—bitter-sweet memories of days gone by.

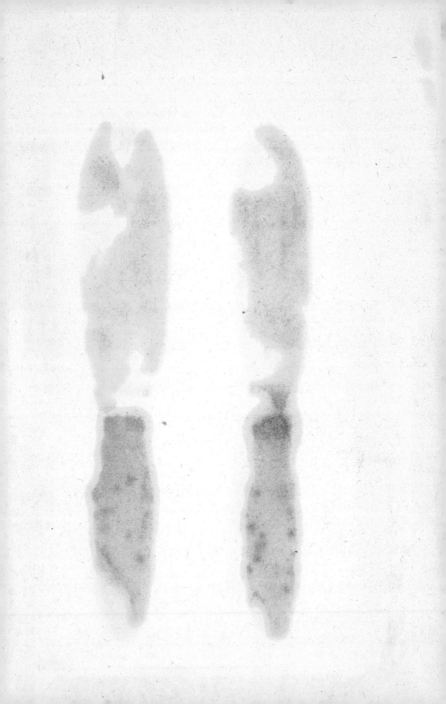

DATE DUE	

GAYLORD   PRINTED IN U.S.A.